T0328689

Cambridge Elements ≡

Elements in Organization Theory
edited by
Nelson Phillips
Imperial College London, University of Alberta
Royston Greenwood
Imperial College London, University of Alberta

ORGANIZATIONAL PARADOX

Medhanie Gaim
Umeå School of Business, Economics and Statistics

Stewart Clegg
*University of Sydney; University of Stavanger
Business School*

Miguel Pina e Cunha
NOVA University Lisbon

Marco Berti
University of Technology Sydney

CAMBRIDGE
UNIVERSITY PRESS

CAMBRIDGE
UNIVERSITY PRESS

University Printing House, Cambridge CB2 8BS, United Kingdom

One Liberty Plaza, 20th Floor, New York, NY 10006, USA

477 Williamstown Road, Port Melbourne, VIC 3207, Australia

314–321, 3rd Floor, Plot 3, Splendor Forum, Jasola District Centre, New Delhi – 110025, India

103 Penang Road, #05–06/07, Visioncrest Commercial, Singapore 238467

Cambridge University Press is part of the University of Cambridge.

It furthers the University's mission by disseminating knowledge in the pursuit of education, learning, and research at the highest international levels of excellence.

www.cambridge.org
Information on this title: www.cambridge.org/9781009124348
DOI: 10.1017/9781009128155

© Medhanie Gaim, Stewart Clegg, Miguel Pina e Cunha and Marco Berti 2022

First published 2022

A catalogue record for this publication is available from the British Library.

ISBN 978-1-009-12434-8 Paperback
ISSN 2397-947X (online)
ISSN 2514-3859 (print)

Organizational Paradox

Elements in Organization Theory

DOI: 10.1017/9781009128155
First published online: September 2022

Medhanie Gaim
Umeå School of Business, Economics and Statistics

Stewart Clegg
University of Sydney; University of Stavanger Business School

Miguel Pina e Cunha
NOVA University Lisbon

Marco Berti
University of Technology Sydney

Author for correspondence: Medhanie Gaim, medhanie.gaim@umu.se

Abstract: Paradoxes, contrary propositions that are not contestable separately but that are inconsistent when conjoined, constitute a pervasive feature of contemporary organizational life. When contradictory elements are constituted as equally important in day-to-day work, organizational actors frequently experience acute tensions in engaging with these contradictions. This Element discusses the presence of paradoxes in the life of organizations, introduces the reader to the notion of paradox in theory and practice, and distinguishes paradox and adjacent conceptualizations such as trade-off, dilemma, dialectics and ambiguity. This Element also covers what triggers paradoxes and how they come into being while distinguishing latent and salient paradoxes and examining how salient paradoxes are managed. This Element discusses key methodological challenges and the possibilities of studying, teaching and applying paradoxes. It concludes by considering some future research questions left unexplored in the field.

Keywords: paradox theory, organizational paradox, competing demands, organization theory, dilemmas

ISBNs: 9781009124348 (PB), 9781009128155 (OC)
ISSNs: 2397-947X (online), 2514-3859 (print)

Contents

1 Background

This Element is written as an invitation for readers who want to become familiar with approaches to organizational paradox theory as a significant aspect of current management and organization studies. The Element introduces readers to the basic understanding of paradoxes, how they are experienced differently and how they are studied. The Element targets doctoral students within management and organization studies in general and faculty at early stages of exploration of paradox theory. For those readers interested in continuing their exploration, there are texts that are more specialized in specific areas of paradox theory, such as Smith and colleagues' (2017c) handbook, two volumes of the Research in the Sociology of Organizations series (Bednarek et al., 2021a; Bednarek et al., 2021b) and Berti and colleagues' (2021) introduction. Our goal in this short Element is to whet our readers' appetite for thinking about paradox and to offer a general overview of its theory for an audience new to the topic. The Element offers a foundational understanding of key terms in the theory as a way of studying organizational life and outlining areas of future research.

Paradox serves as a lens, one among many, that can be applied to organizational life. It sees this life in realist terms, as contradictory and tension-filled. As a lens, paradox provides a way of seeing evident contradictions in organizational life in areas such as leadership, design, innovation and employment relations. It serves to analyse the nature and implication of tensions at individual, group, organizational and inter-organizational levels. As a perspective, it offers a distinct approach compared to the classical management approaches based on 'one best way of doing things' and the contingency approach based on 'if-then'.

Paradox theory in our hands is a lens, yielded sociologically, attuned to the complexity and plurality of interests that organization combines, one theoretical consequence of which is to see contradictions as an unavoidable aspect of doing organization and being organized. Paradox scholars argue from both a theoretical stance and research findings that contradictions seemingly solved rarely are resolved; hence, they are less concerned with solving contradictions. Instead, they are interested in exploring how organizations might embrace, navigate or live with paradox, to use well-known formulations. As a lens, paradox may be combined with other imaginative approaches to explore organizations as contradictions. Using a paradox lens, contradictions are not signs of organizations that are not well managed but rather are seen as a normal condition of organizing.

We have structured this Element as follows: we start by conceptually delimiting paradox, drawing its boundaries and distinguishing it from adjacent concepts. We next move from theory to experience in order to render the abstract more concrete and to discuss the role of responses in the construction of paradox. We subsequently highlight central topics normally associated with the study of paradox we believe need further exploration. We conclude by discussing implications for teaching and for management.

2 Introduction

It is becoming accepted that, in an increasingly complex and fast-paced organizational world, competing demands on leaders, managers, employees and their organizations are heightened. They must innovate while preserving tradition, manage the present and be prescient about the future. They should deliver progressive policies with regards to issues such as diversity or ecology while also meeting performance targets and managing exploration of new ideas while efficiently exploiting old ones, to name but a few tensions (Putnam et al., 2016: 47; Smith et al., 2016). As many authors have noted, firms in a market-based economy need to be innovative, agile and entrepreneurial in exploring the potential of their futures while simultaneously delivering reliability, predictability and robust processes in the present. Organizations, in other words, are confronted with dual expectations: they need to be competent in doing one thing as well as in doing its opposite (Farjoun, 2010), such that leadership becomes an exercise in paradox management in the face of the ambiguities and contradictions of organizational life (Cunha et al., 2021; March, 2010).

Choices that are binary are hard enough to manage. Choice is not always between two courses of action, however. If three rather than two options are considered, as happens when organizations are invited to embrace economic, social and environmental goals, the complexity of choosing increases. These challenges confront managers as they are pressured to manage tensions around sustainability (Preuss et al., 2021), tensions between being a global and a local organization (Geppert and Williams, 2006), being agile and robust or fast and slow (Prange, 2021), or managing for the long term and the short term (Slawinski and Bansal, 2015). Many of these tensions display the characteristics of paradoxes. Paradox refers to persisting interdependent oppositions (Schad et al., 2016). Despite the sense of absurdity that manifestations of paradox evoke because of the seeming tensions between their irreconcilable choices, paradoxes are now viewed as an inevitable consequence of organizational complexity rather than a fault or a flaw in organizational design (Lewis, 2000).

It should not be surprising to social scientists (and others) that contradictions are a persistent characteristic of social organization. After all, it was a fairly famous German writer, Karl Marx, influenced by another famous German, G. F. W. Hegel, who taught the many readers of his three-volume opus, *Das Kapital*, that contradictions marked the essence of the new capitalism about which he wrote. All societies and all organizations for whom success in the market is the measure by which they are judged have capitalist institutions at their core. Contradictions are an immutable aspect of capitalism, according to Marx (1976). The logic of pure capitalism, as Marx (1976) analysed, was one of exploitation in pursuit of profit, the appropriation of value as 'surplus value'. When Marx was writing, this could involve people labouring in appalling conditions with scant regard for health and safety, from the age of six years old. Because of changing social attitudes, reformist politicians, union pressures and the efforts of various advocacy groups, pure exploitation with no caveats attached is no longer the logic of capitalism. With the broadening of the mandate that businesses must observe, there have come into existence several competing demands contingent on the increasing need for contemporary organizations to comply with multiple demands (e.g., being financially successful, pursuing social goals, minimizing environmental impacts, navigating political tensions, etc.). While contemporary capitalism is still marked by the fundamental contradictions that concerned Marx (O'Byrne, 2020), it is also characterized by additional contradictions than those between capital and labour. Managers, the 'new class' increasingly mediating between employers and employees, face contradictions almost as a matter of course: they have to manage what are sometimes diametrically opposite goals simultaneously (Gaim, 2017; Putnam et al., 2016; Smith et al., 2016).

Engaging paradoxes successfully has been linked not only to being sustainable and thus surviving in the competitive world, but also to being innovative (Miron-Spektor et al., 2018; Smith and Lewis, 2011), being agile and reliable (Tsoukas, 2018), maintaining a balance between fluid and cemented routines (Rossi et al., 2020) and so forth. Mismanaging paradoxes has various consequences: it can result in small defeats, such as losing face (Gaim et al., 2021), or major problems with sometimes disastrous consequences. The interpretive indeterminacy that characterized NASA's simultaneous engagement with safety and schedules (Dunbar and Garud, 2009) is a case in point. Paradoxes can be especially difficult to manage when power dynamics come into play (Berti and Simpson, 2021). The challenges that managing paradoxes produces are contingent on the intensification of organizational pressures framing everyday managerial and executive consciousness to pursue seemingly simultaneous but conflicting objectives. These tensions and contradictions are unavoidable implications of organizing (Lewis, 2000; Smith and Lewis, 2011), as well as being challenges to tackle. Moreover, through the realization of their essential nature, a novel paradigm is afforded with which to study organizations (Lewis and Smith, 2014).

The ways in which actors' consciousness experiences and frames paradoxes are assumed to be linked (Beech et al., 2004; Gaim and Wåhlin, 2016). In general, how we make sense of social realities depends on our consciousness, how that has been formed, the metaphors and language embedded in our 'natural attitude' (Schutz, 1967). The stress on consciousness is a fundamental aspect of critical phenomenological approaches (Berger and Pullberg, 1966), which have been incorporated into management and organization studies (MOS) as an emphasis on sense-making (Weick, 1995). Berger and Pullberg (1966) stress the role that objectification and reification can play in the constitution of consciousness. For managers to be aware of contradictions, first these have to become objectified and visibilized (Tuckermann, 2019); where these contradictions are constituted as immutable oppositions between the choices that must be made, then objectification becomes reification. Reification refers to the stabilization of processes as 'things' assumed to have an objective material existence. Being objectified creates a dualism in which choice appears to be the appropriate action: for instance, in tension caused by a conflict between two objective situations, the option is usually posited as either fight or flight. Conventionally, the tendency has been to choose between seemingly paradoxical options by framing the choice between them as an 'either/or' decision (Putnam et al., 2016). Either-or approaches presume a reified state of consciousness, in which the predominant choices are seen to be between phenomena regarded as absolute, determinate and objective. Organizational actors tend to be oriented towards consistency in and of outcomes (Martin, 2007), notwithstanding the complexity and variability of contexts and contingent factors. It is organizational actors' cognitive dispositions that conventionally induce them to seek certainty or to simplify a complex reality (Bartunek, 1988).

Less conventionally, organizational actors are seen to seek simultaneously to engage with both demands, based on the 'both-and' approach (Gaim and Wåhlin, 2016; Miron-Spektor et al., 2011a). The both-and approach is more attuned to the positive social construction of reality in regarding consciousness not as confronting reified objectification but as a process of constructing, deconstructing and reconstructing meaning, engaging with the flow of events and being in a world whose fundamental unknowability is always open to surprise. More processual and positive approaches to paradox are premised on being in the flow of consciousness and constructions, rather than being subject to the choice of one objectified dualism over another, risking reifying one horn of the dilemma while neglecting the other.

Engaging with such competing demands and managing them successfully has been linked with innovation, survival and sustainability (Miron-Spektor et al., 2018; Smith and Lewis, 2011), while mismanagement can create vicious circles (Tsoukas and Cunha, 2017), loss of face (Gaim et al., 2021), missed synergistic opportunities (Smith et al., 2016) and even paralysis and confusion (Ashforth, 1991), especially when power dynamics that impose loss of agency come into play (Berti and Simpson, 2021). That organizations are 'rife with paradox' is an expression that describes the omnipresence of contradictions in organizations, not as aberrant facts but as inherent facets (see Box 1).

The compresence of multiple demands makes it impossible to pursue optimization strategies oriented to a single objective; multiple objectives must be satisfied simultaneously. Devising a one-best-way arrangement of production factors to maximize one objective, profit maximization, is no longer viable. Organizations have become hybrids that need simultaneously to navigate a plurality of contrasting requirements and objectives (Besharov and Smith, 2014; Gümüsay et al., 2020; Smith and Besharov, 2019) embedded in multiple

Box 1 WHY ARE PARADOXES ABSURD SOMETIMES?

In everyday language, paradox is often interpreted as something absurd, lacking sense. In such a perspective, logical arguments in isolation, when joined together, produce some absurd results (Lewis, 2000). Why does this happen? One explanation lies in the fact that organizations, being complex, end up producing contradictions. For example, these can be expressed as contradictory rules. Sometimes these rules need to be disobeyed to be obeyed ('Be autonomous!' 'Don't follow the rules'), expressing what Watzlawick and colleagues (1967) called pragmatic paradoxes. These pragmatic paradoxes, when faced by individuals in positions with limited agency, can be paralyzing. Such individuals are confronted with situations of the 'damned if you do, damned if you don't' type. It is these situations that individuals may find paradoxically perplexing. Cunha and colleagues (2019a) discussed an illustration of this when they explored the application of a 'speak up' policy in a pharmaceutical company. In some cases, the policy and the leader's behaviours were aligned, but in others they were not. While members of the organization were encouraged to speak up, they were liable to receive hard criticism if they did so in ways that some managers regarded as inappropriate. In these cases, although individuals were expected to speak up, their speaking up was not necessarily welcome, producing a context that, for some, was more confusing than liberating.

logics. Profit must be achieved, but so must health, safety, well-being, diversity, inclusivity, equity and sustainability objectives, for example (Pradies et al., 2021). These competing demands have unavoidable implications for organizing (Lewis, 2000; Smith and Lewis, 2011) by complicating the challenges organizations must address and resolve. They are not either-or choices; investors and social expectations assume that *both* inclusivity, diversity, equity *and* profitability and all the other logics that businesses must attend to, as well as profitability, will be managed.

Realization of choices that cannot be optimized by either-or strategies but in which consideration *both* of one option *and* the other affords a novel paradigm with which to study organizations (Lewis and Smith, 2014). Paradoxes can be managed not just as either-or choices (in which it is easy to make the wrong bet by concentrating resources on one 'horn' of a dilemma), but as something that can be handled by both-and strategies that seek to embrace seemingly dichotomous choices in an overall strategy that paradox theorists refer to as 'both-anding'. It is important to note, however, that managing tensions and hybridizing organizations is complex and dynamic, which means the art of managing paradox is a work in progress, never fully achieved, rather than a state that can be obtained on a permanent basis.

In this Element, we explore organizational paradox theory. We present paradox as a meta-theoretical perspective (Lewis and Smith, 2014) for theorizing and as a lens to analyse the nature and implication of tensions in organizations. As a meta-theoretical perspective, paradox (compared with the contingency perspective) can be deployed as a primary or a secondary theoretical lens in MOS, helping to make sense of managing and organizing as an exercise of articulating contradictions at multiple levels of analyses. From a paradoxical perspective, paradoxes exist at the level of *individuals*, such as in sustainability-related identities (Kiefhaber et al., 2020) or creative individual approaches to work (Miron-Spektor et al., 2011b); in dyads, namely leadership duos (Raffaelli et al. 2021); in *teams* (Silva et al., 2013); in the logics underpinning *organization* (Ashforth and Reingen, 2014) and in *inter-organizational systems* such as value chains (Brix-Asala et al., 2018; Schrage and Rasche, 2021). Paradox can be used to complement other approaches (e.g., contingency approach) of organization featuring the potential presence of synergy but also trade-off (Li, 2016).

With such goals in mind, the Element is structured into four main sections. Section 3 introduces the reader to the notion of paradox in theory and practice. We explore what paradox is and what it is not. We distinguish paradox and other close conceptualizations such as trade-off, dilemma, dialectics and ambiguity.

To give the reader a foundation, we discuss the main ontological and epistemological assumptions in paradox theorizing. We cover paradoxical roots and traditions from the East, the West and beyond. Section 4 covers how organizational members experience the tensions in terms of how paradoxes are approached and the available repertoire of responses. We also show how paradoxes are experienced differently and the conditions within which paradoxes are framed and managed. Section 5 focusses on how paradoxes have been studied and the potential areas to consider. We outline a range of possible topics and themes that we believe could further develop paradox theory. In addition, we cover key methodological challenges and possibilities in, for and of studying paradox. Section 6 focusses on teaching and applying paradox. We cover the different pedagogical possibilities and how paradoxes can be applied in practice.

3 Understanding Paradox

Competing demands, such as exploration and exploitation (March, 1991), can be framed in several ways, often with overlapping features, introducing a degree of analytical ambiguity, a problem that risks generating a 'conceptual malaise' in MOS (Putnam et al., 2016: 132). To address this problem, we combine earlier (e.g., Achtenhagen and Melin, 2003; Cameron and Quinn, 1988) and more recent efforts (Fairhurst and Putnam, 2019; Gaim et al., 2018 and 2016; Putnam et al., 2016; Schad et al., 2016) to clarify the terminology used to describe oppositions emerging in organizations. As noted previously, paradox incorporates three core elements (Schad et al., 2016), as depicted in Table 1: opposition, interdependence and persistence.

Graphically, these elements have been depicted in various ways, often with reference to the yin-yang symbol (see Box 2).

A requirement for engaging with paradox theory is clarifying the conceptual boundaries between paradoxes and concepts that are seen to be constitutive of them, such as contradiction, dialectics, dilemmas, tensions and trade-offs (see Table 2). These concepts, although distinct, may be more entangled than our definitions suggest. This occurs for different reasons:

☐ Processes are dynamic, evolving, always on the move, meaning that tensions that are framed as paradoxical can produce dialectical syntheses. These processes occur over long periods of time (see Farjoun (2019), and Hargrave and Van de Ven (2017) to explore the topic further), and the transformation may be difficult to articulate. In other words, in processes that unfold over long periods of time, such as achieving sustainability (Bansal et al., 2018), change may be difficult to follow.

Table 1 The building blocks of paradox

Element	Explanation	Relevance
Opposition	Denotes the presence of elements that seem mutually opposed – such as planning and improvisation or stability and change.	The most salient feature of paradox is opposition, which characterizes the presence of elements whose simple existence is challenging because they give a different prescription for action (Gaim et al., 2018). Their presence is also challenging, given the human propensity to 'solve' dissonance because we find dissonance discomforting (Festinger, 1957).
Interdependence	Expresses the fact that the elements that exist in opposition are also mutually dependent: we understand one element because of our understanding of the other.	The paradoxical view establishes that oppositions are not always mutually exclusive. In the case of paradox, contradiction comes together with interdependence, suggesting that the elements in tension imply one another – they are two sides of the same coin.
Persistence	Denotes the fact that interdependent elements cannot be solved by choice of one or another. For example, the tension between exploring and exploiting cannot be solved by picking one side.	Paradox cannot be solved: it must be navigated or managed. Navigating paradox means organizations need to find dynamic ways of articulating and engaging oppositions.

BOX 2 YIN-YANG AND OTHER WAYS OF REPRESENTING PARADOX

The Taoist symbol of the yin and the yang incorporates all the dimensions of paradox discussed previously in this Element: two forces, both of which contain the seeds of the other and that persist dynamically, as the way of the world. The philosophy of paradox is evident in Lao Tzu's *Tao Te Ching*, for example, in an extract of a poem called 'Paradoxes':

> Nothing in the world
> Is as soft, as weak, as water;
> Nothing else can wear away
> the hard, the strong,
> and remain unaltered.
> Soft overcomes hard,
> weak overcomes strong.
> Everybody knows it,
> Nobody uses the knowledge.
>
> (Translated by Ursula K. Le Guin, 2011: 78)

Thus, in the Chinese philosophical tradition embodied by the yin-yang symbol, paradox is not just a phenomenon that occasionally surfaces. Rather, it expresses a fundamental epistemic principle, the idea that it is 'impossible to conceptualize an idea without considering and incorporating its inverse' (Chen, 2008: 297). It also implies a process ontology according to which entities are connected in a larger system in a continuous process of circular change (Li, 1998). Embracing such a perspective means to acknowledge fully 'the coexistence of true opposite elements in the same place at the same time' (Li, 2016: 322). This orientation appears more 'radically paradoxical' compared to Western thinkers who are influenced by the Aristotelian principle of non-contradiction, which privileges 'either/or' solutions (Li, 2016). For example, coping with paradox by separating poles (Poole and Van de Ven, 1989) or oscillating between them (Lüscher and Lewis, 2008) implies that the opposites remain distinct and independent. Yin-yang presupposes instead an 'either/and' view according to which 'contradiction cannot be resolved and [has] no need to be resolved' (Li, 2016: 48), thus acknowledging that paradox simultaneously includes trade-offs and synergies (Li, 2021).

While thought-provoking, the idea that opposites cannot be separated and that all phenomena should be understood holistically is not without difficulties. The lack of a well-defined methodology to operationalize the concept might make it obfuscated and unfalsifiable (Li, 2014). Indeed, even if the yin-yang symbol appears with increased frequency in the literature, it risks becoming a purely decorative metaphor, one that has lost its capacity to suggest new meanings (Berti, 2017).

Table 2 Key terms and their meaning

Term	Definition
Contradiction	'Opposites that are interdependent but mutually exclusive' (Fairhurst and Putnam, 2019).
Tension	'Stress, anxiety, discomfort, or tightness in making choices, responding to, and moving forward in organizational situations' (Putnam et al., 2016: 71).
Dilemma	'Simultaneous presence of two equally (un)desirable goals/ requirements that cannot be achieved simultaneously' (Putnam et al., 2016: 73).
Trade-off	'A gradual exchange between two demands where more of one means less of the other' (Gaim et al., 2018, p. 5). It is a situation in which 'superior performance in one competitive objective is gained primarily by lowering performance in another' (Da Silveira and Slack, 2001: 949).
Dialectic	'The continuously unfolding triadic process of change through the transformation of a thesis-antithesis into a synthesis that will compose the thesis for a further tension' (Berti et al., 2021b).
Paradox	'Persistent contradictions between interdependent elements' (Schad et al., 2016: 10).

☐ People may use erroneous language and metaphors to describe and analyse phenomena. For example, if what are really paradoxes are taken as dilemmas or vice versa, their essential nature may be misunderstood, leading to undesirable outcomes (Gaim et al., 2018). The frame with which competing demands are seen affects the language used to represent their relationship, which affects how they are made sense of.

☐ Words and theories can have performative effects (Marti and Gond, 2018); because of this, inadequate words may produce undesired effects. For example, contradictory goals cannot always be integrated. As a result, organizations may engage in impossible tasks akin to squaring circles. When this happens, problems may occur, as with Volkswagen's attempt to integrate impossible technological opposites of 'clean diesel' (Gaim et al., 2021).

These attempts at definition may suggest that paradoxes are empirical phenomena that can be somewhat ambiguous. The main problem would then be not to confound them with analogous but distinct concepts or types of tensions (see Table 2). Situations that do not comply with the definition of paradox that we have provided as a state of being in opposition, interdependence and persistence are often described as if they were paradoxical. For example, in the organizational literature, the term 'paradox' has been often used to label phenomena that seem puzzling or counter-intuitive, as in the 'paradox of meritocracy' – that is, the observation that supposedly meritocratic organizations are still gender biased (Castilla and Benard, 2010: 543) – or in the 'Abilene paradox' where people end up acting in contradiction to what everyone really wants to do (Harvey, 1988).

Conversely, authentic paradoxes might be concealed by the label chosen to represent them – for instance, in organizations in which the pursuit of multiple extreme 'stretch' goals (Sitkin et al., 2011) can induce organizational elites to impose absurd demands that are impossible to comply with. If these paradoxes are construed as manageable challenges by elites but as trade-offs by those who had to materially accommodate the demands, it creates a saying-doing gap, a recipe for disaster (Gaim et al., 2021). In terms of competing demands, in these situations, some observers might see organization members as dealing with paradox while others might not. Such representational confusion means that, in practice, when faced with demands such as incompatible and impossible stretch goals, organization members have no clear guidance as to whether to attend to them separately – across time and space – or simultaneously. Thus, how competing demands are framed and responded to is relevant in theory and practice. Before delving into framing, let us present the paradoxical roots and the ontology of paradox, relevant to our understanding in general and the way competing demands are framed specifically.

3.1 Paradoxical Roots

Schad (2017) traces the roots of paradox theory to two philosophical traditions – one from 'the East' and the other from 'the West' – both of which inform normative and prescriptive lenses for studying and dealing with paradoxes (Smith et al., 2017b).

Historically, the Balkans, as the crossroads of the world's civilizations, played an extremely important role as a source and conduit of ideas. It was here that Aristotle formulated the principles of formal logic, giving rise to an either-or system in which oppositions are fully separated (see Gaim and Clegg, 2021; Li, 2016). Ford and Ford (1994: 760–1) explicate three axions associated with formal logic as (I) *contradiction*: that a thing cannot be itself and something else; (II) *identity*: that a thing is equal to itself; (III) *excluded middle*, where a thing is one of two mutually exclusive things (e.g., 'A' or 'Not A') and that thing cannot be both or something in between. These proved to be highly durable foundations for logical thought. Within formal logic, in epistemological traditions in the West, there is an 'absolute and full separation of opposite elements' (Li, 2016: 46) because they are mutually exclusive (Li, 2016). Paradoxes are, therefore, anomalies to be solved by favouring one pole of the tension at the expense of the other. In such a tradition, 'solving' the tensions is a sign of efficiency as the tradition cultivates intolerance to a contradiction (Keller et al., 2017).

Elsewhere, in early nineteenth-century Prussia, other dominant Western thoughts informed by Hegel's dialectics came to emphasize contradiction and change (see Ford and Ford, 1994). Dialectics recognizes gradual, evolutionary and revolutionary leaps. Dialectically, an entity can be seen as a unity of opposites, meaning a thing can be both A and Not-A (Ford and Ford, 1994: 762). Change can occur through the negation of the previous form, where one opposite supersedes the other. In dialectics, paradoxes are tolerated, albeit temporarily or separated (temporarily and spatially) but eventually rejected.

The classic case of this is Marx's dialectical view of history in which each stage of development of the modes and relations of production resolves some contradictions from that which preceded it, leading to the dominance of the capitalist mode of production in which the relations between capital and labour would create a revolutionary consciousness among proletarians. That consciousness would see capitalism overthrown and sow the seeds of a teleological future in which contradictions would be overcome. Thus, central to the West-inspired tradition is a persistent tendency to aim at reducing complexity and uncertainty, striving for simplicity and certainty (Li, 2016).

In Eastern traditions, paradox is the norm, regarded as acceptable rather than as an irregularity (Li, 2016; Schad, 2017). Hence, the traditions embrace complexity and uncertainty (Li, 2016: 49) and accommodation of contradiction is embedded (Keller et al., 2017). Schad (2017: 30–1) recaps key Eastern-based traditions promoting a middle way in which opposition is regarded as empowering.

Although Ubuntu is overlooked in mainstream theorizing, Gaim and Clegg (2021) recently presented it as an Afrocentric view that could inform paradox management, a view that conforms to neither Eastern nor Western orthodoxies. In fulfilling insights 'across paradigms' (Schad, 2017: 28), the Afrocentric view complements the Western and Eastern traditions and adds to our repertoire, contributing to our understanding of paradoxes and paradox management. Ubuntu is based on a humanist premise that aims at a high degree of harmony. It is characterized by focussing on the big picture and continuity (Gaim and Clegg, 2021). Most importantly, it is based on 'otherness', meaning it 'puts others at the centre of concern' (Gaim and Clegg, 2021: 40). Difference and tensions are encouraged, a value in dialogue. Continuity and emphasis on harmony mean the individual and the community are inseparable in that 'there is no individual without community or community without the individual' (Gaim and Clegg, 2021: 41). Consensus is sought through striving to reconcile opposing views. See Table 3 for a comparison of the three paradoxical roots.

Different traditions inform both our theorizing and our practice; thus, we argue for exploration of various traditions because differences in history, institutions, cultures, habits and traditions can clarify the relationships between paradoxes and their contexts.

3.2 The Ontology of Paradox

Another issue relevant for our understanding of paradox is ontological traditions. Discussion of ontology refers to the nature of paradox. In the literature, scholars take two competing views on whether paradoxes are inherent or socially constructed (see Putnam et al., 2016). Contradictions might emerge from the plurality of logics, objectives and meanings. Smith and Lewis (2011) argue that paradoxes are both inherent and socially constructed. They contend that paradoxes exist within a system and are socially constructed through actors' cognition or rhetoric. They propose that paradoxes, 'opposing yet interrelated dualities[,] are embedded in the process of organizing and are brought into juxtaposition via environmental conditions. In this way, we focus on forces that render latent tensions salient to organizational actors' (Smith and Lewis, 2011: 388).

So the question of whether paradoxes exist out there or if they become salient only through social construction is not conclusively answered (Schad and Bansal, 2018). Answering such a question and the clarity that comes with it is relevant to theory development, according to Hahn and Knight (2021: 363), because 'it guides important questions regarding the ubiquity of paradox in organizational life, when organizational actors experience paradoxes, and the

Table 3 Three paradoxical roots (adapted from Gaim and Clegg, 2021: 40)

	Western approaches	Eastern approaches	African approaches
Focus and expected outcome	Single 'Truth,' based on facts and logic aiming for efficiency and performance.	Compromise and achieving the middle way.	Humanness, harmony and continuity.
Difference and tensions	Are an anomaly.	Are a norm.	Are a value in dialogue.
Fundamental tenet when facing tensions	Choice of one over the other. There is one best/right way.	The mean balance and integration between the two poles.	Achieving consensus with the big picture in mind through the understanding of the need of others and building harmony.
Predominant approach	Either-or.	Either-and.	'Both-anding'.
The self and the other	Major concern for self.	Concern for both self and others.	Otherness (a major concern for others).
Understanding of the firm	Collection of individuals.	Wholeness of interdependent opposites.	Group-centred interest.

appropriate way to conceptualize management responses' (Hahn and Knight, 2021: 364). In this section, we present the two major explanations – paradox as inherent to the real and paradox as socially constructed – as well as the emerging bridging views.

3.2.1 Paradox As 'Inherent'

The inherent view treats paradox as belonging to the domain of the real, as a phenomenon whose causal powers will become manifest, regardless of people's cognition. In this interpretation, paradox lies in the domain of the socio-material world. The emergence of contradictions is an inherent feature of complex systems, as discussed by authors in the tradition of systems theory (Boulding, 1956; Katz and Kahn, 1978; Stacey, 1996). The complexity of these systems is a source of contradictions. For example, complex systems comprised of highly specialized agents need a measure of integration (Lawrence and Lorsch, 1967). Yet specialization often makes integration difficult to achieve, as attested by the persistence of organization 'silos' (Tett, 2015). Consider the relationship between change and stability: systems are in constant flux, change being the natural state; yet a measure of stability is needed to allow organizations to gain efficiency, to improve processes and to avoid the syndrome of change fatigue (Bernerth et al., 2011). In summary, the lack of change is as problematic as the excess of change, constituting a change-stability duality (Farjoun, 2010).

Systems' complexity is seen as real-constitutive and the conflicting nature of those systems that create paradox is stressed. These systems are themselves composed of complex agents (Simon, 1996) whose competing goals necessarily produce divergence and contradictions that need to be tackled simultaneously – for example, as change and stability (Farjoun, 2010) or as exploration and exploitation (March, 1991). The tensions between these forces are structurally rooted as inherent features of systems that emerge from the very complexity of the system itself (Schad and Bansal, 2018). The lack of balance in the management of these tensions sometimes becomes manifest in processes such as the lack or excess of change (Langley et al., 2013), too little or too much innovation (Martin, 2009) or competing goals and world views that originate in silos or thought worlds (Leonard-Barton, 1992). Managing paradox involves viewing tensions between elements as dualities rather than dualisms. Duality refers to seeing two elements as opposite sides of the same coin, as the 'twofold character of an object of study without separation' (Farjoun, 2010: 203). Dualism also involves 'doubleness' but in more independent ways, such as oil and water, which do not mix but can coexist. They have no synergy. Paradox management consists of using the synergies between opposite elements as a source of organizational development. It is important, though, to avoid confusion between paradoxes and dilemmas as they require distinct treatment (as displayed in Table 2).

In the inherent view, paradoxes originate in the domain of the real (Bhaskar, 1977) and exist regardless of their being observed, understood or constructed as paradoxes. Paradoxes sometimes become apparent when social totalities manifest contradictions between current and alternative possibilities (Benson, 1977). These contradictions materialize at some point and become visible, for example, in class conflicts or gender relations. In this perspective, the roots of paradox belong to the domain of the real, in the tangible world of socio-materialities composed of contradictory elements such as class, gender or any form of intersectional conflict between identities structured in real experiences of the world. When latent causal powers or propensities become manifest, paradoxes result from the frictions occurring. When treated as real, paradox is anchored in the world of phenomenal things – bodies and their relations with each other and with the actants of organizations, the socio-materialities and structures framing them.

As persistent processes, paradoxes may be latent and take place in the absence of clear cause-effect chains. For instance, gender relations were of little cognitive account for management theorists in the era of the so-called organization man (Whyte, 1956), although class relations were recognized as being organized largely through pattern bargaining by organized labour (Levinson, 1960). Today, the situation is reversed as the liberal political economy has reduced the salient identity of class relations and made gender relations an enhanced identity concern.

To sum, in the inherent view, paradox can be approached as materially real. The role of the organization in this perspective consists of decision makers being alert to the contradictions inherent in the real and investing in their recognition (Knight and Paroutis, 2017; Tuckermann, 2019). The role of leaders is to expose and handle the contradictions that permeate the socio-materialities of organizational life and to tackle them as a source of organizational vitality (Takeuchi et al., 2008).

3.2.2 Paradox As 'Socially Constructed'

In an interpretivist view, paradoxes are socially constructed. People intersubjectively categorize contradictions perceived as paradoxical in reality. Taken-for-granted realities are produced via interaction (Fairhurst and Grant, 2010). Organizational actors 'construct' their reality according to the 'psychological frameworks' they have 'evolved to make sense of' rather than 'perceiving' some objective reality (Eden et al., 1981: 40). These frameworks are more properly thought of as categorization devices that are inscribed in the language and metaphors conventionally in use in specific arenas of action. While these may become psychologically embedded as a normal form of cognition, their origin is decidedly social, lodged in public language rather than private psyches.

From an interpretivist perspective, reality is not some objective truth waiting to be discovered but a product of cognition, discourse and social interaction, leading to the coexistence of multiple realities in contests for legitimacy. Paradox is an 'in-the-eye-of-the beholder' type of phenomenon (Fairhurst and Grant, 2010). According to this perspective, people attribute paradoxical qualities to the complex realities with which they engage. Reality itself is not paradoxical unless framed as such. For this reason, an event that is paradoxical for some observers might for others represent normality or absurdity.

From an interpretivist perspective, paradoxes are a product of human practice and communication rather than realities outside the realm of cognition, an idea that has been central to discussions by authors such as Putnam and colleagues (2016) of how actors in practice construct paradoxes through communication. In this perspective, paradoxes are not produced by isolated individuals but through interactions made possible by public language shared, developed and legitimized by social relations (Hengst et al., 2019). In this view, a paradox is not revealed and made manageable unless it is constructed and made visible (Tuckermann, 2019) through practice.

Given that paradoxes are intersubjective accomplishments (Sharma and Bansal, 2017), they can be 'talked into existence' (Lindberg et al., 2017: 175). That, from the materialist perspective, they might be real does not necessarily render them transparent, explicit (Metcalf, 1940) or visible (Tuckermann, 2019). For this reason, the social construction of a phenomenon as paradoxical should be taken as a deliberate and effortful endeavour. In summary, paradoxes are products of human practice *and* communication where actors construct them communicatively in practice.

3.2.3 Bridging Views

The interpretivist view tends to emphasize sense-making and ignore tensions inherent in the coexistence of competing institutional logics or those that derive from attempts to extract unlimited value out of a resource-finite world (Schad and Bansal, 2018). Moreover, if paradox were purely a product of interpretation, almost anything could be regarded as paradoxical, including situations that can be solved by simple choices: as Luhmann (1995: 360) noted, 'even Buridan's ass, placed, as it were, between two equally tempting bales of hay, will survive, even if it notices that it cannot decide, for that is why it decides nevertheless'.

Similarly, a fully *inherent* view misses the role of psychological defences, time horizons and spatial constraints within which sense is made. Smith and Lewis (2011) suggested that paradoxes are *both* inherent *and* socially constructed. In their view, a perspective that treats paradoxes as real phenomena pays too little attention to the role of interpretation and sense-making. They also argue that, in organizational contexts, contradictions can be construed in different ways (e.g., as an irreconcilable dualism or as a synergic duality). Thus, both individual cognition (Miron-Spektor et al., 2011a; Miron-Spektor et al., 2018) and collective interpretive frames (Keller et al., 2020; Keller et al., 2017) shape the experience of tensions. The sense-making processes that allow recognition of tension as paradoxical and amenable to both-and solutions (Carton, 2018; Hahn et al., 2015; Lüscher and Lewis, 2008; Sparr, 2018) can also be orchestrated by management to make specific organizational actors responsible for managing complexity (Knight and Paroutis, 2017).

Hahn and Knight (2021) articulate a hybrid view of paradoxes using a quantum theory metaphor, arguing that paradoxes exist as an inherent propensity, in a latent probabilistic state, which becomes salient (thus real and enacted in a specific context) through 'observation', which makes them both inherent and socially constructed. Observation refers to a socio-material process of enactment that collapses paradoxes' probability function, making them salient as concrete, specific challenges (Hahn and Knight, 2021). For instance, in social enterprises, contradictions deriving from paradoxes' 'hybridity' are always possible (Battilana and Dorado, 2010), but decision makers usually deal with them implicitly, finding ways to balance social and economic objectives (Gümüsay et al., 2020). Only in some circumstances do these contradictions become concretely manifest as paradoxes – for example, when the choice of sacrificing sustainability for profit causes reputational damage undermining the firm's revenues (Hahn and Knight, 2021).

Another possibility for bridging the two views is performative theory. A performative view posits that paradoxes are produced through words, concepts and categories that reflect a pre-existing socio-material order. These framings have the potential to change this ordering. To do so, appropriate and felicitous conditions need to be met, namely a correspondence between material contradictions and the ideational world as paradoxical. For paradoxes to be managed, they need to be acknowledged and identified. In some sectors and areas, such as sustainability, tensions may be easier to acknowledge than others, given public pressure and scrutiny (Joseph et al., 2020).

Seeing organizations as paradoxical is fundamental for managing them as paradoxical. As Boldizzoni (2020: 158) observed, 'it is the degree to which ideas appear to be compatible with the reality of the moment, rather than any assessment of their overall consistency, that makes them appear plausible to us'. Tensions deriving from conflicting objectives (e.g., maximizing efficiency and being customer-oriented) and trade-offs (e.g., between pursuing flexibility and imposing control) can become inherent to organizing; thus, they become a fundamental ontological feature of social reality since any attempt at simplifying and organizing their existing complexity is bound to generate further complexity (Luhmann, 1995, 2018). However, the manifestation of such tensions as paradoxes is not a 'natural' process. For example, balancing the trade-off between flexibility (required for adaptability and learning) and control (necessary for ensuring standardization and behaviour alignment) is shaped by power relations, as well as by the tensions between different forms of organizational knowledge and practice, vested in different spaces and levels in organizations. Repeated practices naturalize some language categories as normal, thus making them a legitimate way to construe and manage situations (Berti and Simpson, 2021).

A performative perspective allows a description of the processes through which the political dynamics of enactment may turn probabilistic tensions into salient paradoxes. Enactment denotes the process of experimenting and learning while doing. Ideas, things and environments are thus invented and subsequently made sense of through feedback (Farjoun et al., 2015). From this perspective, inherent tensions can take multiple forms when they become manifest as paradoxes. First, they can become seamlessly 'absorbed' in language and practices, as in the case of a surgeon who must cut into the body of a patient in ways that cause hurt to ease suffering. Despite the persistent compresence of interdependent and contradictory requirements (Schad et al., 2016), such a situation will not be perceived as paradoxical but as a taken-for-granted part of the medical lifeworld (Husserl, 1965 [1935]) shared by both the patient and surgical roles, a shared understanding that is mutually constituted while also being embedded in and widely understood in broader social circles. A second possibility is that a paradox *is* collectively recognized as such, and actors collaborate to find flexible ways to cope with the situation, articulating a sense-making process that allows the discovery of new possibilities for action, turning the paradox into a learning opportunity. Third, the situation can become pathological if actors are 'stuck' in rigid positions that impede discursive possibilities. Being stuck may result from an incapacity to accept tensions in knowing or from a lack of agency in coping with what is being known (Berti and Simpson, 2021).

3.3 Latency and Salience of Paradoxes

As highlighted earlier in this Element, central to the theorizing of paradox is its ontology – that is, is paradox inherent in organizational systems or do organization members construct a situation as paradoxical in their representation and sense-making? In practice, the question is whether paradoxes are latent or salient.

Latency and saliency are two important topics in the paradox literature. Not all paradoxes are visible (Tuckermann, 2019) or salient to all actors (Knight and Paroutis, 2017). Tensions that are embedded in organizations (e.g., between exploration and exploitation or between integration and differentiation) may well remain latent (Smith and Lewis, 2011). Untriggered, their dormancy awaits detection (Tuckermann, 2019); hence, their recognition cannot be taken for granted (Knight and Paroutis, 2017).

While there is consensus around the idea, initially introduced by Smith and Lewis (2011), that tensions inherent to organizing are persistent but that their saliency is situational, views diverge around the process that triggers saliency. Some accounts privilege 'exogenous' factors such as environmental conditions of change and resource scarcity (Smith and Lewis, 2011) and/or the presence of particular mindsets and cognitive frames (Miron-Spektor et al., 2018; Smith and Tushman, 2005). Others highlight endogenous factors such as leadership decisions aimed at making middle managers aware of the necessity to reconcile contradictory requirements (Knight and Paroutis, 2017) while still other views focus on processes through which contradictions are continuously made visible and invisible, enabling organized action (Tuckermann, 2019).

There are different views also in relation to the stability of the outcomes of this surfacing of paradoxes. Some accounts suggest that once detected or socially constructed, paradoxes remain salient (Jarzabkowski et al., 2013; Jay, 2013; Lüscher and Lewis, 2008). Other sources propose a more dynamic picture. According to Smith and Lewis' model (2011), effective coping can stimulate innovation but also render the tension less salient. Analogously, Tuckermann (2019) argues, in line with Luhmann's (1995) view, that by alternatively making paradoxes visible and invisible, the organization can avoid paralysis.

Central to the discussion of latency and saliency is that paradoxes might be latent for some while salient for others across a hierarchy. Given their position, managers might see paradox at a higher level while organizational actors are entrenched in their own demands. In addition, the level of salience could also be different because organizational actors might experience the tension of the same paradox differently (see the discussion on intensity in Section 4.3).

3.4 Framing Competing Demands

Once salient, how the tension that constitutes competing demands is framed dictates how it is responded to. Framing is the process by which a phenomenon becomes defined as such and such a type of issue because of the way that it is seen through a set of concepts and theoretical perspectives that delineate what is taken as reality. For instance, the ways in which competing demands are framed implies assumptions about the relationships between these demands – for example, whether they are oppositional, interdependent (Chen, 2002) or both.

Moreover, different types of framing produce diverse options for organization members' sense-making. So, when the tensions resulting from competing demands become salient, because of either individuals' cognition or materially real factors, how organization members socially construct and make sense of them will vary. Sense-making, in general, is understood as making something sensible (Sandberg and Tsoukas, 2015), and it involves emotional, cognitive and behavioural elements. The cognitive dimension consists of those stable constructs that structure members' categorization devices (Sacks, 1972), providing a lens through which to understand a situation.

Once organizational members face the tension, they draw on typical patterns of cognition, implicit assumptions and prior experience (Miron-Spektor et al., 2011b) to frame it in a way that structures and bounds experience (Bartunek, 1988) as an 'either-or' choice or two legitimate demands that should be accommodated based on 'both-and' thinking, for example. Cognition is, however, just a piece of the puzzle. Organization members also experience different emotions when faced with competing demands. For some, the tension can arouse anxiety and discomfort; others might feel energized as they work through the tension (Ashforth et al., 2014; Beech et al., 2004). These emotional and cognitive dimensions are manifested in and direct organization members' actions (Denison, Hooijberg and Quinn, 1995). As organization members frame competing demands, the emotional, cognitive and behavioural elements are intertwined even though they are presented separately. One cannot be separated from the other, but rather they overlap and interact in the form of a vortex (Coget and Keller, 2010; Gaim, 2017).

In the *classical* theoretical literatures on organization, which 'describe correlations between stable entities' (Hernes and Bakken, 2003: 1517), competing requirements will be dealt with in terms of a decision as to which option is the best to prioritize at the expense of the other, aiming to identify the 'one best way' to optimize the desired outcome. While 'one best way approaches' have declined in influence with the passage of scientific management (Taylor, 1911) into intellectually being a historical curiosity (if not practically), the idea lingered on with the notion of '*contingent* best ways' to organize, depending on context (Donaldson, 1987). More recently, recognition of the increased complexity and fast-changing nature of context has led many theoreticians to foreground organizing processes rather than reify them into structures whose lack of liquidity becomes problematic when change is to be explained (Weick, 1979). Processually, the framing of organizations as becoming, with their structure constantly reproduced (Clegg et al., 2005; Stephenson et al., 2020), is also undergoing change. Framed in this alternative epistemological perspective, both the manifestation and the treatment of competing demands (as a paradox or not) assume a different meaning. These alternative forms of making sense of competing demands and the associated tensions can be enacted in different ways.

When competing demands are framed as *dilemmas*, they become problems to be solved (Li, 2016: 47). Such a situation becomes manifest as an either-or choice, one in which an alternative must be selected at the expense of the other, in a win-lose situation (Ashforth et al., 2014). Dilemmas pose incompatibility between competing demands that necessitate choice as a response (Janssens and Steyaert, 1999; Westenholz, 1993). When choices are made, the tension is considered resolved for once and for all.

Framing competing demands as *trade-offs* stresses their opposition, implying that any gain in relation to one demand requires a sacrifice in relation to the other (Byggeth and Hochschorner, 2006; Gaim and Wåhlin, 2016). However, in this case, the outcome is not binary: it is possible to find a balance between the conflicting but interdependent functional demands (Garland, 2014). Trade-offs can be considered as 'more or less' compromises, where responses must partially attend to one demand at the expense of the other, with a moderate focus on either demand (Achtenhagen and Melin, 2003; Ashforth et al., 2014). Thus, trade-offs imply that more of one means less of the other, forcing organizational actors to settle for a compromise. When tensions are framed as trade-offs, actors predominantly see their conflictual nature, not their interdependence and the energy their intersection can generate.

In cases of dilemmas and trade-offs, organizational actors tend to close off tensions and resolve contradictions. Hence, they might miss the possibility of embracing, engaging and accepting both sides simultaneously. Thus, while both dilemma and trade-off picture a static reality, a *dialectical* perspective (Benson, 1977; Clegg and Cunha, 2017; Putnam et al., 2016) frames oppositions as engines of transformation. The pattern assumes an initial thesis, followed by its antithesis; the dialectic is then resolved through their synthesis (Poole and Van de Ven, 1989; Smith and Lewis, 2011), which becomes a further thesis, and so on. The synthesis incorporates elements of the two contrasting positions but is neither a resolution nor a harmonious reconciliation. First, once the synthesis is achieved, it will be perceived as a new thesis likely to provoke its antithesis and reignite the dialectical cycle (Clegg and Cunha, 2017). Second, dialectics highlights the role of resistance and change through conflict (Hargrave and Van de Ven, 2017): depending on power balance, thesis and antithesis will combine differently (even if both are likely to leave a trace in the synthesis).

When competing demands are framed as *paradoxes*, they are seen as dualities, opposites that coexist, as necessary elements of a unified whole (Smith and Lewis, 2011). For this reason, they are persistent and cannot be 'resolved'; despite their opposition, they are interdependent (Schad et al., 2016; Smith and Lewis, 2011). When these contradictory elements are constituted as equally important in day-to-day work, organizational actors frequently experience acute tensions in engaging with these contradictions (Cunha et al., 2002; Gaim et al., 2018). When framed as paradoxes, the competing demands are seen as contradictory and interdependent and the resulting tension is persistent, not resolved.

Thus, when we frame a process, we decide what to see and what not to see. Moreover, our framing informs our response, meaning how we deal with a tension depends on how we frame it and the language or metaphor we use to represent it. When framing competing demands, conceptual clarity is important because framing is associated with how tensions are interpreted. Moreover, conceptual clarity makes the connection between framing and responses clearer (Gaim et al., 2018). Given the complex and changing nature of organizations and organizing, competing demands will be framed differently across time and space. Thus, conceptual clarity allows organizational actors to 'recognize the consequences of shifts in their practical consciousness when iterating between dilemma and paradox or between dilemma and duality, for instance' (Gaim et al., 2018: 11) and to recognize different framing of competing demands and their implications. If aware of the different framing, organizational actors can deliberately examine transitions or iterations among different forms and how they are treated.

For researchers, conceptual clarity helps to study patterns between different framings and responses and why and how such changes occur, answering questions such as: Why do actors change their framing? At what point? What was the trigger? How does their sense-making shift? Doing so will open a space for process-oriented longitudinal studies in different contexts.

4 Experiencing and Responding to Paradoxes

As highlighted in Section 3.1, organization members' responses to paradoxes are linked to the ways in which they are framed (Beech et al., 2004; Gaim and Wåhlin, 2016). Organizational members strive to make sense of and respond to paradoxes except where they ignore them – voluntarily or involuntarily. When made salient, paradox produces significant relational and emotional pressures

(Patrick, 2018). On one hand, a paradox can provoke anxiety and frustration and be a source of organizational paralysis and tugs of war (Smith and Berg, 1987). Paradox can lead to confusion and powerlessness, with people confronted with requests that are 'paradoxical' in the sense of being absurd. In this case, the adjective refers to something that makes no sense. Examples of this expression abound when formal organizational rules contradict other rules or when bosses invite their subordinates to be more autonomous but reserve for themselves the right to make the final decision. It is in this context that paradox corresponds to its popular meaning of something that is nonsensical, even absurd.

On the other hand, paradox can generate energy and function as a source of creativity (Beech et al., 2004; Gaim et al., 2022; Miron-Spektor et al., 2011a). Paradoxes' double edgedness is reflected in this capacity both to perturb established certainties and release untapped creativity (Gaim, 2018; Schad et al., 2016: 6). Hence, how organization members respond to paradoxes depends on how they are framed. Linked to framing is how organization members make sense of paradoxes and the approaches they use to do so (Putnam et al., 2016). As organization members face competing demands that organizations confront simultaneously, either in the same space or time or across time and space (Poole and Van de Ven, 1989), various coping strategies are possible based on either-or or both-and approaches (Martin, 2007; Putnam et al., 2016). Responses can be defensive (i.e., aiming at removing or 'solving' the contradiction) or active (i.e., attempting to harness the contradiction to create productive outcomes) (Jarzabkowski et al., 2013).

4.1 Approaching Paradoxes

Individuals arguably prefer consistent outcomes (Martin, 2007) because their cognitive dispositions induce them to seek certainty or simplify a complex reality (Bartunek, 1988). When faced with competing demands, conventionally, individuals' tendency has been to choose between options by framing the choice as an 'either/or' decision (Putnam et al., 2016). Either-or approaches presume a reified state of consciousness in which choices between phenomena are seen as absolute, determinate and objective. Less conventionally, organizational members are seen to seek to engage both demands simultaneously, based on the 'both-and' approach (Gaim and Wåhlin, 2016; Miron-Spektor et al., 2011a).

The both-and approach is attuned to the positive social construction of reality in regarding consciousness as a process of constructing, deconstructing and reconstructing meaning, not as confronting reified objectification. Reality is constructed through those creating it engaging with the flow of events and being in a world in which events happen whose fundamental unknowability is always open to surprise. Processual and positive approaches to paradox are premised on being in the flow of consciousness and construction. These approaches do not treat meaning as subject to a choice of either one side of an objectified dualism or another, risking reifying one horn of the dilemma while neglecting the other.

The literature on paradoxes (details in Putnam et al., 2016; Schad et al., 2016) covers two dominant (i.e., *either-or* and *both-and*) and one emerging approach (i.e., *more-than*). In the *either-or approach*, paradoxes are resolved by fully separating opposites whose differences are accentuated. Approaches – as they are tied to how organization members respond – are important because organizational members' perceptions often obscure the relatedness of the options that paradoxes elicit (Lewis, 2000). Similarly, Smith and Berg (1987: 208) argue, 'it is important to keep in mind that survival and growth in a world of contradiction involve not only the experience of a paradox but the various ways of thinking about the paradox that enables us to tolerate or manage contradiction and conflict'. Furthermore, Cameron and Quinn (1988) note that organization members often impose an either-or approach in treating tensions as dilemmas that could more fruitfully be approached from a both-and approach.

From an either-or perspective, paradox is typically seen as problematic when contradictory poles are regarded as distinct phenomena that function independently of each other (Lewis, 2000). Framing things in this way means that choice must be for either one or the other option. The upshot of paradox being treated as either-or is that once a pole is opted for, actors become defensive in protecting and rationalizing their choice and the other pole is neglected.

By contrast to the either-or approach, a *both-and* approach enables organization members to recognize and become comfortable with, even profit from, paradoxical experience. Through a both-and approach, organization members develop cognitive capability and emotional orientation to accommodate contradictions simultaneously, by zigzagging, by shrinking and stretching, or by integration (Ashforth and Reingen, 2014; Miron-Spektor et al., 2018; Rosales et al., 2022). Typically, this leads to an active engagement with both poles, juggling them and ways of dealing with them in balance.

The *more-than* approach is an extension of the both-and approach. In this approach, competing demands are not merely accommodated, but there is an active search for novel solutions based on creative synergy. The distinction from both-and is that while in both-and there might be a balance of competing demands of social and commercial demands, for example, their relationship is not fundamentally altered in a novel way. According to Putnam and colleagues (2016), more-than responses connect oppositional pairs that make up the paradox, moving outside of them or situating them in a new relationship. The early phases of the construction of the Sydney Opera House epitomize such a dynamic where members holding contradictory interests appreciated the importance of 'others', which gave rise to 'a collaborative expansion in which members abandon polarity and instead experimentally examine ways of embracing both in their pursuit of the aesthetic moment' (see Gaim et al., 2022). In the both-and and more-than approaches, experiencing paradox is seen as a generative process, a source of energy, in which poles that are paradoxical become accommodated through developing novel and creative synergy (Putnam et al., 2016). The process is dialectical, moving from thesis→ antithesis→synthesis in a constant flow of becoming, generating new insights and transformations.

We have now established that how organizational members respond (e.g., actively or defensively) to paradoxes depends on how paradoxes are approached (Putnam et al., 2016). The relationship between approach and response is not necessarily linear. Certain approaches may not necessarily result in a corresponding response; nonetheless, we can argue that, under normal circumstances, approaches are tied to how organizational members respond (Martin, 2007). We have summarized how the approaches are tied to responses in Table 4; the movement from defensive to active portrays the increasing sophistication in the way tensions are responded to from simple choice to engaging both simultaneously.

4.2 Repertoire of Responses to Paradoxes

As shown in Table 4, there is a range of responses within the different approaches. Smith and Berg (1987) have produced fundamental work cataloguing a repertoire of group responses to paradoxes. In their work on group life, the authors highlight the fact that individuals experience ambivalence stemming from the simultaneous wish to be both 'a part' of the group and 'apart' from the group. First, this occurs when a group responds to paradox by resisting or by being unwilling fully to explore painful and distressing aspects of their experience of paradoxes (Smith and Berg, 1987: 211–12), often leading to them seeking a middle ground to make the contradiction seemingly disappear (Smith and Berg, 1987: 212). Second, organization members might attempt to eliminate the contradiction through a competitive instinct, pitting members' opposing reactions to it against each other to see which proves stronger or more powerful (Smith and Berg, 1987: 212). Third, organization members might overlook contradictory elements by failing to recognize the contradiction by seeking consensus through 'putting aside' polarizing differences (Smith and Berg, 1987: 213–14). The attempt to compromise, eliminate and overlook, however, can lead to 'stuckedness' (Vignehsa, 2014), what Hage (2009) refers to as a form of existential immobility, the condition now popularly known as

Table 4 Approaching and responding to paradoxes

Approaches	Either-or			Both-and
Grand response	Defensive		Active	
Actions actors take	Avoid.	Choose.	Accommodate.	Connect.
Description	Blocking the awareness that tensions exist or refusing to recognize them.	Choosing or favouring one demand at the expense of the other based on one-sided power dynamics.	Recognizing tensions and attempting to accommodate competing demands but not in their full strength.	Understanding of complex contradiction, tension and ambiguity as natural conditions of work.
Repertoire of responses	Repression and denial (Lewis, 2000).	Suppression (Jarzabkowski et al., 2013); reaction formation (Lewis, 2000); compliance (Jarzabkowski et al., 2013); opposition (Jarzabkowski et al., 2013).	Ambivalence (Lewis, 2000); spatial and temporal separation (Poole and Van de Ven, 1989).	Synthesis (Poole and Van de Ven, 1989); transcendence (Lewis, 2000); adjusting (Jarzabkowski et al., 2013).

Groundhog Day syndrome. Being in a state of stuckedness keeps members from creating a framework for understanding how their actions prevent productive movement (Smith and Berg, 1987: 210).

Alternatively, Smith and Berg (1987) noted that organization members might engage in movement. Movement results from having the emotional and intellectual engagement to discover how linking oppositional poles can release energy essential for group development. Achieving this sense of movement, doing something, requires immersion in and exploration of polarities and reclaiming emotions and reactions that have been split off by making a choice that involves focussing on either one pole or the other (Smith and Berg, 1987). Reclaiming requires reintegrating opposing or contradictory reactions, acknowledging contradictions rather than eliminating them. Acceptance of contradiction is a necessary but insufficient step; movement necessitates immersion in and exploration of the polarities to enable reframing their relationship. Such reframing brings with it new ways of looking at the opposition (Smith and Berg, 1987: 218).

In another foundational study of the paradox of change processes and organization members' emotions, Vince and Broussine (1996) identified defence mechanisms. Repression denotes blocking unpleasant experiences from memory; regression refers to resorting to action that previously provided some security; projection means transferring personal shortcomings to others; reaction formation is refusing to accept an unpleasant reality (Vince and Broussine, 1996: 5). Based on both Smith and Berg (1987) and Vince and Broussine (1996), Lewis' (2000) seminal work recapitulates the repertoire of responses into paradoxes. In attempting resolution, organization members reduce frustration and discomfort, which initially produces a positive effect. However, Lewis (2000: 763) notes the initial positive effect will eventually foster opposite, unintended consequences that intensify the underlying tension. Managing that taps paradoxes' positive potential may be difficult, as it requires radically rethinking past perceptions and practices. To do so successfully, managers must recognize, become comfortable with, even profit from, tensions and the anxieties they provoke.

Building on these and previous works, Jarzabkowski and colleagues (2013) categorize responses to contradictions as either 'active' or 'defensive'. Similarly, Lewis and Smith (2014) classify the range of responses as 'strategic' or 'defensive'. Conceptually, categorizing responses as active or strategic as opposed to defensive captures the polar emphasis of short-term and long-term orientations. Active/strategic responses provide organization members with long-term relief and sustainability; the alternative offers temporary fixes. Based on empirical work on paradoxes in telecommunications, Jarzabkowski and colleagues (2013) identify specific responses, including suppressing, opposing and adjusting. Suppressing involves overriding one element of the paradox while fostering the other, as one demand is seen as more important than the other. In opposing, unlike suppressing, both demands are deemed important. However, organization members, rather than realizing the demands as interdependent, pit representations of the opposition against each other, forcing one or the other representation to the margins. In adjusting, organization members recognize the opposites as interdependent objectives each of which must be achieved (Jarzabkowski et al., 2013: 253–5). Both suppressing and opposing institute salience and latency with respect to the poles of the paradox. The conceptual repertoire of responses has been advanced by Schad and colleagues (2016), who address individual and collective responses to paradox. More recently, Clegg and Cunha (2017) have categorized the repertoire of responses to paradoxes based on excluding, separating, integrating and connecting.

These repertoires of responses show the several ways organizational members deal with paradoxes; some lead to positive outcomes while others do not. Some lead to virtuous cycles while others create cycles that are vicious. When organization members seek to resolve paradoxical tension, vicious reinforcing cycles play out; where they capture the enlightening potential of paradoxes, their positive aspects are tapped. Thus, one possible outcome of paradoxes as persistent phenomena is the emergence of cycles or circles.

These circles reveal the repetitive nature of organizations when some organizing logic prevails that is difficult to abandon. Success, for example, can lead to circularity (perhaps virtuous and subsequently vicious) as organizations repeat well-tested responses. When organizations repeat a solution that worked well in the past, they can prolong their success, deepening an architecture of organizational simplicity (Miller, 1992), but one day, while the environment will have changed, potentially the organization will repeat the past recipe. This partly explains why successful organizations stumble even when their competitive intelligence tells them that dangerous moves are being tried by competitors (Vuori and Huy, 2016). Circles may become so ingrained that the attempts to correct them and change course can aggravate their dynamics: the solution becomes part of the problem. For managers, the implication is that organizations sometimes need to zoom out to make sense of their relative position, over time, in dynamic environments. A response that led to a sustainable outcome might not work if organizational conditions have changed or if the nature of the paradox has changed, for example, in its intensity.

Typically, our discussion of responses has focussed on a single paradox. A paradoxical tension rarely comes alone, nor is it dealt with in isolation, in reality. Organizational members deal with multiple paradoxical tensions mostly interwoven and nested at different levels (Andriopoulos and Lewis, 2009; Sheep et al., 2017). For example, in addition to exploration and exploitation, organization members might be dealing with social and commercial paradoxical tensions. Paradoxical tension at one level, for example, a commercial and artistic paradox at organization levels, affects the passion and discipline paradox at an individual level (Gaim, 2018). There are also paradoxes within paradoxes, for example, coopetition for sustainability (Manzhynski, 2021). When competitors collaborate in sustainability projects, multiple tensions (cooperation and competition, knowledge sharing and knowledge protecting, common and private goals, economic and environmental) are evident (Manzhynski, 2021). Thus, although most of our examples entail single paradoxes, the reality is far from that simple. Paradoxes are experienced not in isolation but rather as interrelated and at multiple levels.

4.3 Not All Paradoxes Are Created Equal

Although the different responses imply that paradoxes are being dealt with differently, the focus remains on the presence or absence of the oppositional poles – that is, paradoxical versus non-paradoxical. There is little theoretical or empirical evidence demonstrating whether all paradoxes are experienced with the same intensity. In the literature, the issue of intensity is implied but not theorized, although it is significant to understand the responses. Thus, in addition to the issues of saliency and latency (explained in Section 3.3), response to paradox also reflects intensity, meaning that paradoxes are dealt with differently. Both-and-related responses take different forms depending on how intensity is considered. In other words, when constructed as paradoxes, their intensity might differ both in time and space. For example, Raisch and colleagues (2018) show how organization members' maturity changes the way they represent a paradoxical tension. When organization members learn enough about a paradoxical tension, their understating increases through time. As a result, the intensity of the experience of a particular paradoxical tension might vary.

Thus, the simultaneous presence of contradictory yet interrelated demands does not mean both demands are equally relevant or that they are dealt with with equally high intensity, for example, across levels. The question of intensity raises an important point: not all paradoxes are constructed equally because the intensity of the experience of paradoxes can be very different depending on the context in which a paradox becomes salient.

For example, the tension between planning and improvising may be salient when plans fail and something must be done urgently to solve a problem

(Cunha et al., 2003). In a different context, a senior physician in an emergency room might feel the tension between flexibility and compliance or autonomy and control differently and less intensely than a novice physician (Rosales et al., 2022). The issue of intensity is more noticeable in the context of gender. In general, while both men and women face similar paradoxes in organizations in their roles as organization members, normative expectations make the experience of the relation between working life and life more generally, the work-life paradox, a more intense experience for women often putting in a 'double-shift' (Baxter et al., 2008; Padavic et al., 2020) of unpaid domestic as well as paid employment duties, when childcare, meal preparation, cleaning and shopping are included in domestic responsibilities that all too often are gender assigned. If we take a gender perspective on work-life balance, irrespective of gender, those with access to more resources have many more options to lessen the intensity of the work-life paradox by the simple practice of hiring others to do the home-life work. Opportunity maps on to gender and gender maps on to segmented labour market participation. Female workers in secondary, unskilled segments of the labour market have far less economic opportunity to contract out much of domestic labour compared to their sisters in the primary segment.

When it comes to accommodating competing demands, the intensity of the paradox experienced by those acting in and on it is thus of relevance both theoretically and in practice. The experience varies with familiar aspects of structural intersectionality in social and organizational life (McCall, 2005). Thus, in addition to the consideration of latency and saliency, exploring intensity can enrich the conceptualization of paradox. It has been long noted that 'strength' of presence, in addition to the simultaneous presence of contradictory demands that constitute paradox, should be considered in studying paradoxes (Clegg et al., 2002: 494).

The intensity of experienced paradoxes can be conceptualized as the extent to which an actor experiences a set of interdependent and contradictory requirements as more or less salient, impactful and difficult to tackle. The notion of paradox intensity comprises three different dimensions. First, *contradiction intensity* refers to the relative attribution of importance to the contradictory poles by actors experiencing paradox. While both poles may be accommodated, they are not necessarily equally important to the observer.

Second, *impact intensity* refers to the variable extent to which actors recognize contradictory demands in terms of urgency and consequence. To what extent is it considered urgent for the actors to respond to the paradox? What is the magnitude of consequence of productively (or not productively) responding to paradoxes? Thus, impact intensity is seen in terms of the timescale of perceived urgency and the perceived magnitude of response in relation to organization performance. Whether the threat/opportunity offered by the existence of the contradiction is affecting the organization in the short or long term depends on the politics of representation and temporality.

Third, *challenge intensity* refers to the degree to which response to the paradox is available/possible for the actors experiencing it. Intensity will be at its peak when actors lack the capacity to cope with the paradox, as is often the case with pragmatic paradoxes that paralyze actors with pathological consequences (Berti and Simpson, 2021). Material conditions and power relations, as well as the discursive availability of accounts grounded in different professional identities, will shape the degree to which a paradox is experienced as a challenge that can be met. Thus, when responding to paradox, in addition to the issue of salience, the intensity of paradox experience adds the needed complexity into the theorizing and closes the gap between theory and practice.

In the case of the latter, one issue missing in paradox theorizing is boundary conditions. True, the theoretical development has developed our understanding of paradox and how to deal with them. However, with the proliferation of studies on paradox there is a tendency to take paradoxical framing as a panacea. When focussing on the positive aspects, disregarding the challenges of paradox management could widen the gap between theory and practice (see Box 3). To fill that gap, we now turn to boundary conditions.

5 Studying and Exploring Paradox

Paradox theory has progressed enormously in recent years. Paradoxically, however, one might say, the more we know, the more we know what we don't know about paradoxes. The discovery of areas of collective ignorance, alongside the questioning of the taken-for-granted assumptions that ground theorizing, are essential parts of theory construction. In this section, we present possible avenues for expanding and advancing paradox in both our research and our teaching. This is no easy task, as paradox is a challenging idea.

Paradox may constitute a 'new normal' (Gaim, 2017), but its normality does not render it easier to understand, teach or apply. While the paradox literature has developed around a clear and coherent conceptual 'core', several issues remain open. These constitute both a challenge (for the coherent development of the theory) and an opportunity (for fostering new avenues of inquiry and application).

First, the notion of paradox is used in a very broad manner to label interdependent tensions that have different degrees of 'paradoxicality' in the sense of creating situations of quasi-impossible choice. Some paradoxical tensions are

> ### BOX 3 THE PROBLEM WITH WIN-WIN
>
> As a practice that favours both-and rather than either-or thinking, paradox may be regarded as the domain of win-win approaches. Win-win, however, must be seen as difficult navigation of oppositions. As King and Pucker (2021) have observed, 'win-win' can be taken as a pain-free approach to problems. The difficulty, however, is that pain-free ideas tend to be simplistic solutions to complex problems.
>
> To make things even more complicated, simple, well-intentioned solutions often aggravate the problems they intended to solve (e.g., consider the case of microcredit, as Beck and Ogden (2007) elaborate). Gender equality strategies may aggravate gender imbalance (Padavic et al., 2020), empowerment may disempower (Collins, 1994), changes intended to increase both quality and efficiency can be neutralized by an entrenched bureaucracy (Cunha et al., 2019), quality management may increase rigidity and reduce quality. In other words, complex systems have unintended effects that cannot be anticipated. Such systems, linked by supply chain, contacting and other devices of intermediation, are complex and attempts to reduce such complexity to simple metrics will frequently not only fail to achieve what they were designed to achieve but will introduce more rather than less complexity.

more amenable to resolution: this is the case of tensions between multiple logics (e.g., between social, environmental and financial goals). Others – as is the case for pragmatic paradoxes (Berti and Simpson, 2021) – are more difficult to tackle, entangling actors in absurd, intractable predicaments since any attempt to address one pole of the tension will complicate the other and no balance is possible, as in the case of a front-line employee who is both required to give all their attention to each customer and forced to deal with multiple clients who demand attention.

Second, researchers have insisted that paradoxes are often nested (i.e., one level informs other levels) and interwoven (i.e., one tension affects other tensions; see Cunha et al., 2017). While these attributes render paradox appealing as a topic for research, making it challenging, cutting across levels of analysis and rich in systemic effects as well as incorporating an element of surprise, it also makes it difficult to analyse, compare and formulate practical recommendations about their management.

Third, using the term 'paradox' to describe organizational tensions and oppositions may disconcert many practitioners, who often perceive these situations as normal challenges rather than logical puzzles. The relationship between paradox and cognate concepts should also be clarified. Other disciplines, such as economics or strategic management, usually describe contrasting requirements in terms of trade-offs, situations that require finding a balance between conflicting functional demands (Garland, 2014), or where a scarce resource can be invested either one way or another. Defining the relationship between trade-offs and paradoxes would help to communicate with other disciplines and facilitate the application of paradox theory to management practices.

Despite these difficulties, paradox seems to be in the process of becoming a mainstream topic in MOS. Researchers can claim a classical lineage for some of their ideas because some influential paradoxical ideas, such as creative destruction, are well established. Intellectually establishing a lineage or genealogy for ideas is remote from them playing a constituting role for acting paradoxically as a managerial panacea. In this section, we discuss how paradoxes can be studied. We explore current challenges, possible research avenues and methodological challenges and possibilities. The following section focusses on how paradoxes can be used pedagogically.

Given paradox theory's immaturity, other domains could also have been considered. For this reason, we invite our readers to add to our themes others that may contribute to the future development of paradox theory in line with personal interests. In doing so, we highlight possible avenues for the expansion of paradox theory. Expanding and critically analysing the theory of paradox is important for both conceptual and practical reasons. In conceptual terms, paradox theory is a recent stream in MOS, as witnessed by important onto-epistemological debates.

5.1 Onto-epistemological Aspects

Given the performativity of theories, paradox theory needs to be interrogated because of its potential to inform practice. We start with onto-epistemological aspects that will influence the subsequent sections. The theoretical foundations of paradox theory are still being debated. It is generally accepted (see, e.g., Smith and Lewis, 2011) that paradoxes are both inherent to reality and socially constructed (resulting from human thinking and acting). These two perspectives leave some questions open, however.

Accepting that paradoxes are anchored in the domain of the real, in the complexity of social systems (Benson, 1977), means that whether people 'detect' them as real or not, they will be real in their consequences. For this reason, research on the material contradictions that precipitate paradox constitutes an important research endeavour. Despite not framing some conditions as paradoxical, paradoxes will sometimes reveal themselves as inconsistency, incoherence or absurdity. When fundamental contradictions operating in the domain of the real are not acknowledged, organizations may be surprised by the revelation of problematic inconsistencies, as happened with Volkswagen (Gaim et al., 2021). In other words, when organizations try to make the impossible possible, they may end up confirming that reality is not infinitely malleable.

Future research may thus continue the analysis of the ontology of paradox. Hahn and Knight's (2021) work on the quantum view of paradox offers a useful step in this discussion, exposing the role of a measurement apparatus in the emergence of paradox as a salient. In this sense, paradoxes are not 'out there' to be discovered/detected but are enacted. In this perspective, enactment necessarily comprises a creative constitution of reality from the potentiality of the superposition state. A state of superposition refers to the peculiar circumstance in which particles seem to be in two or more places or states at once. Physicists have found this an almost impossible state to measure because the act of measurement requires an experiment that makes the condition under investigation disappear. The experiment involves firing photons at two parallel slits in a barrier. Tiny particles can behave like waves, with those passing through one slit interfering with those going through the other. Oddly, this interference occurs even when only one particle is fired at a time, seemingly passing through both slits simultaneously, interfering with itself and disappearing. Quantum researchers face the paradox of not being able to know exactly what a superposition is without looking at it. However, the very act of making it visible makes it disappear.

The situation is in reverse in organizations. Organizations generate potential but indeterminate paradoxes that can become salient to actors as *real* experiences following an act of measurement (Hahn and Knight, 2021). It is only when measured that one can determine the state the organization is in, meaning there is no object to detect prior to measurement. Measuring constitutes the object. To the measurement, we can add an enactment apparatus. An enactment apparatus explains why paradoxes are performed (or not) in the way people label contradictions.

Another implication of the distinction between latent and salient paradoxes is the idea that power relations are always implicated in the social construction of paradox. As Huq and colleagues (2019) argue, paradox needs to be 'protected' to avoid the vested interests that support one of the opposite poles overwhelming the other. Moreover, depending on the available words used for labelling – given the circumstances and their position in power circuits – people may create paradoxes as sources of revitalization or may become entrapped in pragmatic paradoxes (Berti and Simpson, 2021). Thus, people create paradoxes by responding to contradictions and the many possible responses (Berti et al., 2021b) are indicative of how different conditions favour various responses. Some people use humour (Jarzabkowski and Lê, 2017) while others use silence (Cunha et al., 2019b); for others, conformity and acceptance of organizational inconsistencies as normal (Ashforth, 1991; Clegg et al., 2016) is the response. Paradoxes can be resisted and contradictions may be crystalized by habitual responses when the condition persists.

Paradoxes are only half the picture; it is what actors do with them, how they respond to them, that is significant. The focus on how paradoxes are created by responding opens a middle way between the constitutive and inherent views. It suggests that new lines of research can be obtained using performative theory (Marti and Gond, 2018) as well as via pragmatic and realistic views. A performative view, one that looks at how paradoxes are enacted, may help to bridge inherent and constitutive views and provide a possible avenue to delve into the onto-epistemological aspects of paradox theorizing. Accordingly, future research may study paradox management by considering the measured object and the measurement apparatus as well as the words in use and the enactment apparatus. These are promising lines of research as they may help to explain why paradox may be a source of balance or a part of the absurdity.

5.2 Conceptual Clarity

Difficulties exist with the establishment of the conceptual boundaries of paradox. There is now a widely shared definition of paradox as involving persistent opposition between interdependent elements (Schad et al., 2016), but it is not always easy to discriminate between similar but different types of tensions (trade-offs, dilemmas, dialectics). Therefore, the challenges around conceptual boundaries are still relevant. This is so because conceptual confusion deters theory development given the different representations of tensions (Clegg, 2002); what is 'x' might be treated as 'y' depending on the features employed to conceptualize it. Thus, conceptual clarity can avoid what Putnam and colleagues (2016) call conceptual 'malaise'.

Moreover, conceptual challenges are aggravated by the fact that contradictions have many faces and may change over time (Gaim et al., 2018). For this reason, paradoxes may metamorphose to become concepts with different characteristics. For example, the paradoxical tension between thesis and antithesis may at some point originate new solutions which transcend the current forces, establishing a new thesis for a new cycle (Clegg et al., 2002; Farjoun, 2016; Smith and Lewis, 2011). Thus, there is still a need for more research on conceptual clarity because framing competing demands as 'x' or 'y' required a substantive feature.

Recently, a formal way to assess the 'strength' of paradox has emerged in philosophy. Starting from the definition of paradox as a set of mutually inconsistent claims, each of which appears to be true, Margaret Cuonzo (2014) has proposed considering the *subjective probability* of each claim (and of their conclusion) as a measure of the intractability of paradox. Subjective probability is the degree to which a rational observer believes something, where 0 stands for complete disbelief and 1 for complete certainty, with each intermediate value representing an increasing level of probability. Since the observer making the claim is assumed to be rational, subjective does not mean arbitrariness but is based on available information and judgement; hence, it does not imply that the claim is correct or true. What creates the paradox, in the perspective of the observer, is the presence of two interrelated claims that – taken separately – each on its own has a very high degree of subjective probability; however, taken together, they lead to a conclusion that has a very low degree of subjective probability. In other words, 'the greater the disparity between the subjective probabilities of the claims and the final conclusion, the stronger the paradox' (Cuonzo, 2022: n. p.). For instance, the classic liars' paradox ('this sentence is false') is a very strong paradox since it can be broken down into a set of claims with almost perfect subjective probability (if the sentence is false, then it is true; if the sentence is true, then it is false; sentences can be either true or false), leading to a conclusion that has zero subjective probability (the sentence is both true and false).

The same principle can also be applied to organizing paradoxes, which can reveal different degrees of strength. For instance, the tensions between exploitation and exploration are often described as a paradox (exploration requires learning, which implies trying new things, which reduces efficiency; by contrast, exploitation requires control and standardization, which reduces innovation opportunity). Yet, the subjective possibility of the claim 'exploitation hinders exploration' (and of the converse) is far less than one: it has been shown that innovation can be found in preserving traditions, that ambidextrous balance is possible, that innovation may produce long-term efficiency, etcetera. Conversely, social contexts can generate very deep paradoxes such as the 'paradox of tolerance' (Popper, 2012), the idea that a tolerant society must be intolerant of intolerance. In this case, all the claims that form the paradox have a very high degree of subjective probability (to be completely tolerant, society must allow the expression of all views; also intolerant views are views and as such should be freely expressed; but expression of intolerance creates further intolerance, betraying the principles of open society), but lead to a conclusion that would have zero subjective probability (to be completely tolerant, a society must allow the creation of intolerance). This paradox is more than a logical puzzle since it is at the basis of very concrete and contemporary debates such as regulation of social media expression (should people be free to spread misinformation, 'alternative facts' and/or xenophobia?).

In the context of organizational paradoxes, the situation is further complicated by the fact that tensions between inconsistent claims are not just linguistic puzzles. Organizing is founded on language, the most basic form of organizing of experience; thus, meaningful statements cannot be made outside of a language game (Wittgenstein, 2010). Therefore, the subjective probability of a claim is socially constructed. By making information available to different organization members, limiting their judgement and decisional autonomy and setting decisional rules and routines, organizations strictly regulate the formation of subjective probabilities.

Thus, the intensity of organizational paradoxes becomes a function of the way in which organizational design and practices give priority and credence to claims (e.g., 'one must always abide by laws' and 'maximising profit is an absolute priority') which, in some situations, are inconsistent (the need to pay a bribe in order to secure a contract). Interestingly, the solutions logicians propose to treat strong paradoxes, such as keeping statements about facts and statements about statements (meta-statements) distinct (Berti, 2021), are often not practicable in an organizational context. In organizations, actors who are subject to contradictory requirements that are made paradoxical by constraining rules (as in the case of pragmatic paradoxes) are not the same people who review rules or redistribute resources (the organizational equivalent of 'meta-communicating'). Examining further both the conceptual and empirical intensity of organizational paradoxes using the lens afforded by the notion of subjective probabilities offers a promising avenue of inquiry.

5.3 Conceptual Straightjackets

As in any theorizing, some contributions tend to stick. Thus, in order to counter the premature convergence of paradox as noted by some (Cunha and Putnam, 2019), paradox theory may avoid the use of previous theory as a straightjacket and instead explore novel possibilities. The most obvious acceptance of the previous theory, given our own experience as authors and reviewers, refers to the repetition of the four types of paradoxes enunciated by Smith and Lewis (2011) (see Box 4) as probably the best example. In this repetition, the power

> BOX 4 FOUR CATEGORIES OF PARADOXES
>
> Smith and Lewis (2011: 383) note that 'the four categories of paradoxes represent core activities and elements of organizations'.
>
> ☐ **Learning** (knowledge) paradoxes surface as dynamic systems change, renew and innovate where organization actors deal with the decision to build upon or destroy, to engage in radical or incremental innovations.
> ☐ **Belonging** (identity/interpersonal relationships) paradox driven by complexity and plurality brings issues of identity where actors deal with issues of individual versus the collective, homogeneity versus distinctiveness.
> ☐ **Organizing** (processes) paradox emerge as actors deal with cooperation and competition, empowerment and direction, routine and change, control and flexibility.
> ☐ **Performing** (goals) paradox stems from the plurality of actors with divergent goals becomes some are internal and others external to an organization manifested in a goal to deal with financial and societal goals. (Smith and Lewis, 2011: 383–4)

and persuasiveness of the work of its authors is evident, but one consequence is to distract other authors from possible divergent expressions or complementary ones already established in theory. For this reason, instead of accepting well-established ideas, researchers may approach them with a critical stance, following recent developments in paradox theory, despite some aspects of paradox theory converging too rapidly for critical reflection on the language game being created (Cunha and Putnam, 2019).

While the four types offer the structure for a macro-level understanding of tensions in organizations, they are too coarse-grained to cover the actual expressions of paradox at the micro level of analysis. Inductive research should thus enter the field without preconceptions about the paradoxes that will be found. Assuming *ex ante* that there are four paradoxes limits the power to induce observations of paradox emergence in organizational settings. It is a constraining acceptance of implicit structural functionalism.

Notions such as a triple bottom line (Hussain et al., 2018) or trialectics (Ford and Ford, 1994) open new and more complex ways of seeing tension and contradiction in organizations. Our invitation to avoid the straightjacket is not meant to suggest that trialectics is 'better' than dialectics or that three-force tension is more sophisticated than tensions between two poles. Instead, we merely invite you to approach the theme without too much preconception: it is still too early to close possibilities.

5.4 Boundary Conditions

Given the proliferation of paradox theorizing, there is a tendency to focus on the bright side, romanticizing the paradoxical approach as a panacea to tensions and contradictions as uniquely creative, generative and innovative (Gaim et al., 2021). Mainstream research usually focusses on the virtues of engaging paradoxes, implying that embracing paradoxes leads to creativity, learning, exceptional leadership, high-performing teams, resilience and long-term performance (Hahn et al., 2018; Miron-Spektor et al., 2018; O'Reilly and Tushman, 2008; Smith and Lewis, 2011). However, managing paradoxes effectively is difficult, costly and precarious (Andriopoulos and Lewis, 2010; Smith, 2014).

Lately, there has been a focus on the dark side of paradoxes (Berti and Simpson, 2021), situations in which mismanaged paradoxes might lead to unintended consequences (Gaim et al., 2021). Such works show the limits of paradox as an approach that, by implication, limits theorizing while also opening new opportunities. If the limitations are ignored with a focus solely on virtues, we risk limiting the development of the field and creating 'narrowness and unquestioned acceptance of existing knowledge' (Cunha and Putnam, 2019). Thus, addressing the limitations keeps research in paradox theory 'vibrant and polyphonic', creating a space for 'divergent views'. Moreover, if unintended consequences are to be managed, not avoided, then we need to consider what it takes to deal with paradoxes.

Divergent views and limitations open a space to explore boundary conditions – that is, conditions that 'place limitations on the propositions generated from a theoretical model' (Busse et al., 2017: 576). Exploring boundary conditions enables us to specify 'under which context a proposed construct will or will not apply' (Busse et al., 2017: 578). For example, we know having a paradoxical mindset or consciousness helps actors to engage with paradoxes. However, there are conditions in which this might not work (see Figure 1). Exploring boundary conditions helps in exposing those limitations and, in doing so, increases the 'explanatory power' of paradox theory and 'increases precision' by specifying how and when it is applicable. Thus, boundary conditions refer to the who, where and when aspects of theory; if the purpose of theory is to describe, explain and predict, then exploring and articulating boundary conditions enables us to explain and predict better (Busse et al., 2017).

To discuss the boundary conditions, let's now consider Figure 1. When triggered or due to unsettling events, latent tensions become salient, necessitating a response. Studies have shown that, once paradoxes are rendered

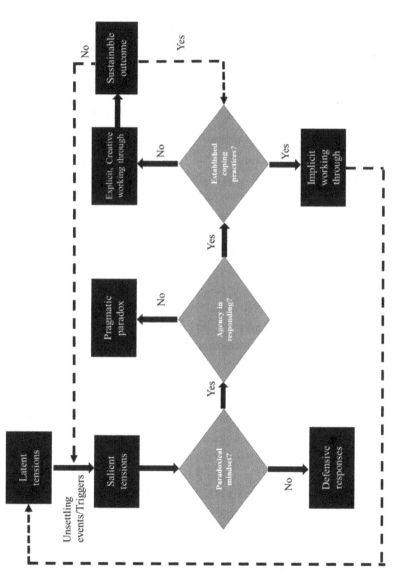

Figure 1 Boundary conditions in paradox theorizing and management

salient and visible, it does not mean organization members will be able to do something about them. This possibility is contingent on the possession of an individual (Miron-Spektor et al., 2018) and collective (Gaim and Clegg, 2021; Keller et al., 2020) *mindset* (a common disposition towards a phenomenon) that enables actors to accept paradoxes and leverage their creative potential. In its absence, actors experiencing tensions are more likely to have negative emotions in the presence of contradictions and have recourse to defensive solutions (such as suppressing one pole of the tension), thus risking igniting vicious circles (Smith and Lewis, 2011).

5.5 Paradoxical Mindset As a Collective Phenomenon

The notion of a 'mindset' may be represented as an individual-level phenomenon, but it may also be approached from multiple levels of analysis. Research may explore the cross-level dimensions of the paradox mindset. The mindset may be an individual attribute (Sleesman, 2019), an inter-individual process (Pradies et al., 2020), an organizational orientation (Takeuchi et al., 2008) or an inter-organizational mechanism, as in experiences with coopetition or supply chains (Schrage and Rasche, 2021). Pamphile's (2021) work on the interpersonal dynamics articulating philanthropy professionals suggests that these may coordinate their sense-making processes to navigate occupational challenges. This study is indicative of the promise of the study of a paradox mindset as a *collective process* and of the need to see paradoxical phenomena at different levels, zooming in and out (Schad and Bansal, 2018).

The notion of a paradoxical mindset has made its way into organizational paradox theory. A paradoxical mindset has been defined as a way of thinking that helps to interpret the experience as involving contradictory features (Miron-Spektor et al., 2018). It predisposes individuals to think about contradictions as normal and integral to reality rather than as signs of absurdity that should be eliminated. Paradoxical thinkers may thus be more prepared to assume that contradictions should be navigated as inter-dependent rather than as dilemmatic either-or types of choices. A paradox mindset thus may favour a world view in which contradiction is normal rather than aberrant. For example, organizations favouring a paradoxical view may see routine and creativity as two sides of the same coin (composing a duality) rather than as a dualism in which elements are mutually exclusive.

Even if actors deploy a paradoxical mindset, if they are impaired in their *agency* in choosing appropriate ways to deal with a paradox, they will experience a pragmatic paradox as paralyzing and pathological, a situation in which contradictory demands can neither be renegotiated nor coped with because any legitimate avenue of action is blocked (Berti and Simpson, 2021). Even if actors are sufficiently empowered to choose a response to a paradox, it is not a given that they will decide to embrace the tension, acknowledging its persistent and interdependent nature. So, if actors are sufficiently empowered, the next question is, are coping practices in place? Sometimes strategies can be 'found' and stabilized if they are perfected over time.

If actors accept that the world is paradoxical and acknowledge that reality can be productively enacted as paradoxical, paradoxes *will* be found. As the old sociological adage has it, if people define situations as real, they are real in their consequences. When paradoxical interpretations are consistently enacted, organizations may acquire mastery in the art of managing paradoxically, thus making paradoxes existentially normal. Strategies can thus be 'found' and stabilized if perfected over time, as happened with Toyota's systematic pursuit of quality and efficiency via a combination of routine and creative improvement (Adler et al., 1999). The practice inspired by the theorizing proves the value of the theory. If repeated, responses become normal and are stabilized as routines or coping practices. A successful paradox *coping practice* can become so entrenched that actors will take it for granted: the paradox is so seamlessly managed that 'working through it' becomes normal, habitual and an implicit act. When situations change, as they do processually, especially when events occur that render existing sense-making problematic, what worked at some point might fail to result in the same outcome, hence creating 'breakdowns' in organization members' response to paradoxes. Breaks in sense-making necessitate new practices. If they try and fail to handle paradoxes, they may revisit the paradoxical terms and 'solve' the paradox by reducing expectations (Li, 2021). Thus, by questioning the dominant viewpoint and exploring boundary conditions, we can complexify our theorizing (Smith et al., 2017a), which will not only foster theory development, but also mitigate the 'research and practice' gap.

As Gaim and Clegg (2021) have noted, the collective appreciation of paradox as a collective mindset may help to explain why paradox becomes ingrained. Paradoxes can also be ingrained in organizations as a cultural attribute, as in the studies by Brown and Eisenhardt (1997) in the computer industry and by Takeuchi and colleagues (2008) and Aoki and Wilhelm (2017) on how Toyota both creates tensions and buffers against tension, studies indicative of paradox as part of an organization's identity and way of doing things. For this reason, exploring the mindset-culture nexus can help to explain how mindset becomes a defining cultural attribute, which may lead to the acceptance of ideas such as 'creative routines' as normal (Nonaka and Takeuchi, 2021).

5.6 Meta-theorizing

Paradox has been touted as constituting a meta-theory (Lewis and Smith, 2014), a theory of theories, or a theory that may be coupled with other theories to tackle their respective elements of contradiction. Understood as a source of overarching perspectives aimed at producing a perspective that transcends organization theory (Ritzer, 1990; Zhao, 1991), this meta-theoretical potential, until now, has been more enunciated than elaborated. In Ritzer's (1990) formulation, an understanding of meta-theorizing represents it as a source of overarching perspectives that are more fundamental than organization theory.

There is ample space to realize this potential by expanding paradox theory as auxiliary to theories of organization, something that has started to occur with institutional theory (Smith and Tracey, 2016), teams (Silva et al., 2013) and hybrid organizing (Smith and Cunha, 2020). The meta-theoretical potential of paradox, however, is not an easy accomplishment. There are several obstacles. Theories tend to be protective of their core (Clegg et al., 2022) and paradox, with its emphasis on contradiction, is not necessarily a common angle for organizational theories more attuned to structural equilibrium than processual contradiction.

5.7 Cross-Cultural Aspects

Organizational paradox scholars have paid limited attention to the cross-cultural dimension, with some important exceptions (Keller et al., 2018), especially those oriented to the study of the Eastern yin-yang approach (Li, 2016). This is regrettable because, if paradoxes can be thought of as socially constructed, then attention needs to be paid to the cultural conditions of paradox, namely to the way different cultures express different preferences. These cultural predispositions may be the source of contradictions about preferences in cross-cultural settings.

For example, 'good leadership' has a very different meaning in various parts of the world (Meyer, 2014). If leadership constitutes itself as a paradoxical practice (Cunha et al., 2021), leading in different contexts may render this paradoxical side salient. Studying paradoxes across cultures can also facilitate the understanding of how different peoples deal philosophically with contradiction (Peng and Nisbett, 1999) as well as how different cultures and world views nurture distinct types of contradictions (Cunha et al., 2019b).

For this reason, instead of accepting that a paradoxical mindset means the same in different places, it might be relevant to explore the different meanings of paradox (e.g., how people understand the contradictions ontologically) and the interpretations of their expressions (i.e., what is the meaning of a 'balanced leadership' in different contexts?). Diverse world views, such as the differences between East and West, have been explored, but the need to integrate other epistemologies, such as African, may also be considered (Gaim and Clegg, 2021). Mapping the geography of paradoxical thinking and practice can thus provide interesting opportunities for the advancement of paradox research.

5.8 Delayed Effects

An important area for further exploration is the study of delayed effects – that is, effects that become visible with a lag, which result from the (mis)management of paradox. It is known that as organizations pursue a purpose, they generate intended but also unintended effects (Merton, 1936). For this reason, even if the paradox is typically portrayed as a source of balance, it is important to recognize and explore the fact that paradoxes can lead in directions other than those that are balanced.

The future expansion of paradox theory may thus explicitly incorporate consideration of the effects that management produces when organizational members either tackle or ignore paradox. An important area will refer to the consideration of delayed effects of paradox. A notable case during the writing of this Element was that of Theranos and its founder, Elisabeth Holmes. What was lauded as a paradoxical mastery of cutting costs while improving quality to disrupt a massive laboratory-diagnostic industry was just a sham and false promises with an implication for how promising start-ups in Silicon Valley are perceived. Similarly, some effects, namely in processes such as sustainability, do not have immediately visible effects, but the compounding factors of contradictory processes need to be studied and understood. Another theme might refer to the consequences of balance: maintaining a system in balance may be devalued as a practice because there will be nothing, apparently, remarkable or significant about it. Therefore, the question, echoing Repenning and Sterman (2001), is to what extent the efforts of managers handling paradox are appreciated for maintaining balance and for solving, by anticipation, problems that never came into existence.

5.9 Methodological Challenges and Possibilities

Apart from these themes, there are also methodological challenges in current theorizing that open possibilities in studying paradoxes. In line with the different onto-methodological approaches, multiple perspectives (see Box 5 for some methodologically exemplary works) may be used to further expand organizational

Box 5 Exemplary research: Methodological directions

Murnighan and Conlon (1991) studied the dynamics of intense teamwork using a sample of British string quartets. The authors used interviewing but also objective data, such as team stability and reviews of the quartet's performances, to associate the way quartets handled paradoxes with their respective critical acclaim and artistic effectiveness.

Miron-Spektor and colleagues (2018) offered a foundational work that employed mixed qualitative and quantitative methods and highlighted the paradoxical mindset as a key to unlocking potential as organizations deal with everyday tensions. They developed a scale, employed it in samples across cultures (United States, UK, Israel and China) and tested it in a US large firm.

Smith and Besharov (2019), in their inductive study of DDD, a social organization operating in Cambodia, combined paradox theory and hybrid organizing to explore the contradictions inherent to social enterprises.

Benbenisty and Luria (2021) used a mixed-methods approach to explore the sensemking of paradox. Conducting their fieldwork in the Israel Defense Forces, the authors combined quantitative and qualitative strategies to discover the strategies people use to articulate contradictory demands in their daily practice.

There is a dearth of work using a quantitative approach. As is normal in a relatively new field, most research is inductive. Inductive work is important to gain a textured understanding of the phenomenon but quantitative deductive work may help to establish a more generalizable theory. Quantitative studies of paradoxes such as Keller and colleagues' (2020) exemplify the potential of quantitative work for generalizable theory.

paradox theory. In this section, we present four methods, two for each of the dominant ontological views. No method is purely focussed on one ontological foundation or the other, but the difference helps to clarify our point. In exploring the socially constructed and material facets of paradox, organizational scholars have different strategies available to them. We highlight discourse analysis, phenomenological approaches, historical methods and system views.

Discourse analysis. Several studies analyse the role of discourse in shaping paradoxes and responses to them. First, competing discourses can be seen as a source of paradoxical tensions, as in the clash between environmental and business goals (Carollo and Guerci, 2018). If the business goal is that of maximizing shareholder value, then the logic of this position may clash with the logic of sustainability. The temporality with which the goals are being accounted is important, however. In the short term of quarterly or annual results, it may well be feasible to minimize expenditure on sustainability to fatten the bottom line. However, in the long term, as investors and customers increasingly single out sustainable products and producers, the value may well decline and reputational capital will be lost, such that it is too late to repair the damage. In the short term, it may be smarter to pursue both profitability and sustainability rather than just one goal. In fact, chasing either goal in isolation could be ruinous. If the goal is sustainability, in an ecological sense, unless value is delivered to shareholders, they are likely to protest and might well divest, with bad consequences for the business. Arguments about shareholder value versus sustainability will be communicated in board meetings, in project scrums, on websites and in announcements. All of these can be analysed *discursively*, identifying what characterizes the discursive themes of different constellations of interest in the organization.

Some discourses may incorporate contradictory requirements that in some conditions become manifest as pragmatic paradoxes, depriving actors of any legitimate action alternatives (Berti and Simpson, 2021) in situations resembling Orwellian doublethink, affecting female workers and managers who are required to perform incompatible gender and professional roles, for instance (Oakley, 2000; Wendt, 1995). Double-bind situations and the paradoxes they cause can be part of a patriarchal culture that politicizes the female body. Organizations often expect female workers to embody a feminine ideal in terms of dress and deportment, manners and language. However, equally, they are usually expected not to display their sexuality in the office or other conventional workplaces. Ferguson (1984: 95) points out that 'Women are not powerless because they are feminine; rather, they are feminine because they are powerless because it is a way of dealing with the requirements of subordination.' The classic example of this is Kanter's (2008) discussion of secretarial gossip in organizations, typified in the TV drama series *Mad Men*. By mentioning or hinting at weak spots in terms of the male superordinate's conduct of office, a little political leverage can be exercised. Gossip about the other has the potential to subvert power or subtly resist it, as well as acting as a safety valve. Managers can rarely avoid being talked about, and gossip is something its subject cannot frame, as it goes on 'behind their back'. Gossip becomes seen as a feminine trait in such organizations, but, as Ferguson points out, it is a tool of the less powerful against the more powerful. Discourse-based paradox studies could also describe how discursive interactions shape paradoxes (Jarzabkowski and Lê, 2017). Discourses can be leveraged to transcend paradoxes (Abdallah et al., 2011) by stretching actors' imagination and mobilizing actions so a new frame of reference can be developed that accommodates the opposites, overcoming their contradictions.

From a methodological perspective, discourse analysis offers fruitful opportunities to study paradoxes because of the diversity of approaches and perspectives about what constitutes discourse and on discourse influence on social interactions (Berti, 2017). Small 'd' discursive approaches that treat discourse as a linguistic performance (Alvesson and Kärreman, 2000) focus on how experiences of contradictions can be diversely construed and described (e.g., as dilemmas, conflicts or double binds) by organizational actors, leading to different behaviours and coping strategies (Engeström and Sannino, 2011). Capital 'D' perspectives instead present a 'muscular' view of Discourses (Alvesson and Kärreman, 2000), as productive of meaning and identity; authors embracing this view typically place discursive interplays as the source of 'real' tension (Francis and Keegan, 2020; Gotsi et al., 2010; Iivonen, 2018). In doing so, they often tap into dominant social tropes.

Conceptually, discourses play a role both in generating systemic tensions and in making them salient to actors (Hahn and Knight, 2021; Putnam et al., 2016). Thus, from a methodological viewpoint, it can be more fruitful to employ a small 'd' discourse perspective to examine the way in which tensions are made visible and collectively made sense of. Doing this entails attending to the local discourses in an organization, those modes of rationality that underlie different discursive strategies and positions, perhaps embedded in disciplinary knowledge bases. Instead, a big 'D' perspective helps to investigate the conflict of logics that cause 'systemic' (Schad and Bansal, 2018) tension, such as would be characteristic of the earlier opposition noted between shareholder value and sustainability as distinct societal level tropes. Fairhurst and Putnam (2019) propose an integrative methodology to bridge these two perspectives, incorporating in the mix a grounded theory approach.

Phenomenological approaches. The lived experience of paradox is an important dimension to explore (Pradies et al., 2021), with paradox often presented as a source of discomfort (Vince and Broussine, 1996). It is possible, however, that paradox also constitutes, in some circumstances, a source of excitement (Gaim, 2018), as reflected in Niels Bohr's famous quote: 'How wonderful that we have met with a paradox. Now we have some hope of making progress.' Phenomenological studies may help to illuminate how individuals experience paradox, not as something abstract, but as a concrete, embodied experience. The same methodological approach may also help to discover when paradox is lived as a positive event, a source of novelty and discovery, the paradox of wonder Daston (2014) discusses.

The paradox of wonder is that it is both the beginning of inquiry as well as the end of inquiry that puts an end to wonder. 'The marvel that stopped us in our tracks – an aurora borealis, cognate words in languages separated by continents and centuries, the peacock's tail – becomes only an apparent marvel once explained' (Daston, 2014). Wonder works as a measure of ignorance; the unlearned experience is frequently that which is rarely learned. Why something is so may be marvelled at from ignorance or known from wisdom. Phenomenological research may thus bring concreteness to paradox as something people experience bodily, as a state of existential indeterminacy, of not knowing. Several organizational processes, such as sensemaking, are often viewed as cognitive or discursive processes, but the connection between the cognitive and the lived (emotional, biological, primal) experience of contradiction may be as important as exploring its meaning. Recent work explores the sense-making of paradox (Benbenisty and Luria, 2021); future research may consider its emotional component.

Historic methods. Longitudinal work may help to introduce granularity into the empirical relationship between paradoxes and processes, such as circles and dialectics. The relationship between these constructs has been studied and it may be interesting to explore what new qualities a paradox in the present might gain when viewed from a historical perspective, a possibility that needs to be further addressed – consider Farjoun (2021) and Hargrave (2020) for important recent developments.

The understanding of these processes will benefit from the recourse to historical methods that may illuminate the unfolding of paradoxical socio-historical patterns over time and space, as organizations and their missions change in response to changing contexts (Pradies et al., 2020). Jarzabkowski and colleagues (2021b) propose the integration of historical and practice approaches to explore how the present and the past intertwine in producing patterns with circular characteristics (consider the case of the practice of the *mita* in Bolivia, as explained in Robinson and Acemoglu (2012), evidencing the deep historical roots of some present-day practices). Historical repetition may normalize contradictions to the extent that they are no longer 'visibilizable' (Tuckermann, 2019). Longitudinal work conducted over shorter periods may also be illuminating, as illustrated by Maclean and colleagues' (2021) analysis of the evolving narratives at Procter & Gamble during a fifteen-year interval, which unearth the dynamic, evolving nature of storytelling around contradictions. A case in point of the latter is the paradox of Afghanistan – frequently invaded, never conquered, a graveyard of imperialisms. The latest ascendancy of the Taliban may seem paradoxical in view of the trillions of dollars spent in the vain pursuit of its defeat (Jenkins, 2021). Historically, it should not (Hallyday, 1996); paradoxically, it was US CIA trillions that helped fund it in the first place as a gambit in the Cold War, the one before the War on Terror. The historical paradox is why Western powers persist in fruitless adventurism somewhere they have never succeeded in the past.

Systemic views. Systems dynamics may constitute a powerful approach to the paradoxical process in a way that will circumvent the limits of cross-sectional studies normally concentrating on a single paradox in a time-bounded way. Systems dynamics methods (Sterman, 1994) place a much greater emphasis on the part-whole relationship, the non-linearities, feedback loops, temporal effects of the functioning of complex systems than do other methods. The fact that agents have a limited understanding of the system mitigates over-optimistic perspectives about paradox and its management. In fact, organizational systems and their environments are often too complex to be understood by the agents operating in them. Thus, studies using a systems view might offer a more complete picture of paradox management than the current theorizing affords.

6 Teaching and Applying Paradox

We now turn our attention to the challenges of teaching paradox and the use of a paradox pedagogy, or as Lewis and Dehler (2000) put it, a pedagogy based on contradiction. We assume that paradox, because of its meta-theoretical quality, can be used as an auxiliary theory to explain phenomena in the domains of MOS. The paradox lens can be used to discuss themes related to fields as diverse as sustainability, supply chains, strategy, leadership, ethics, corporate social responsibility and organizational design. All these areas may benefit from the consideration of the contradictions inherent to designing, organizing and managing organizations.

6.1 Pedagogical Possibilities

Central to the paradox pedagogy is a shift in world view from aiming for linearity and certainty towards embracing uncertainty and ambiguity. Thus, instead of teaching students that the world of management is linear, a world of problems waiting for the correct solution, paradox pedagogy may assist students in understanding the uncertainty and the ambiguities of the world of organizations (March, 2010).

Paradox can be used to expose the role ambiguity plays in management, showing that decisions are always more complex than portrayed in textbooks, that important themes raise important ethical issues and that sometimes decision makers are confronted with what Nayak (2016) called the tragic question, the awareness that confronts leaders with the need to decide between better and worse wrongs. The inevitability of tragedy should not obscure, however, the importance of measuring the consequences of one's actions and the power of paradoxical thinking in weighting one's impact. We envision three pedagogical strategies to use paradox in MOS: reality to theory, theory to reality and theory to theory.

6.1.1 Reality to Theory

Case studies may be used to illustrate the presence of paradoxes in the real world. Actual situations may be examined to discover the presence of competing demands and the implications for management. For example, cases such as McKinsey's involvement in the opioid crisis, putting 'profit over people's lives' (Edgecliffe-Johnson et al., 2021: 17), or the demise of Danone's chief because of his failure to reconcile economic and social targets (Van Gansbeke, 2021), are revealing of what happens when profit is not counterbalanced by attention to economic results. In this case, a paradox is interpreted from the case, as in the VW emissions scandal (Gaim et al., 2021) during which the company promised the US market clean diesel that was fast, cheap and green. The promise was paradoxical as all three could not be realized together and the engineers failed to accommodate the tensions between performance, efficacity and environmental concerns. A similar case includes Silicon Valley's one-time darling Elisabeth Holmes and her health-technology- and medical-laboratory-services firm, Theranos, where the promise was of cheaper, faster and better blood-testing technology, which did not materialize.

Instructors following this strategy may cite recent news to infuse paradox theory with an element of recency and realism. Media reports and journalistic pieces can lead students in the direction of paradox. In this way, cases can facilitate reflection on the paradoxical nature of management and organization, how paradox can be navigated or failed to be navigated and what it requires to do it well.

6.1.2 Theory to Reality

A second approach consists in starting with theory of paradox and asking students to find examples in the media. In this case, real-world illustrations explain paradoxes previously covered in theory. An instructor might explain the fundamentals of paradox theory or some of its elements and ask students to discuss the theory with some illustrative case. For example, instructors may discuss paradoxes in leadership and ask students to bring cases to illustrate them. As of the time of writing, the case of Carlos Ghosn, the famous executive who fell from grace after his leadership of Renault-Nissan came under question for financial impropriety, comes to mind; also, the political case of Boris Johnson, the soon to be ex-prime minister of the United Kingdom who lost the support of his MPs and was forced to resign. The sequence from theory to reality may ground theory in evidence, showing that paradox theory offers a lens that helps to illustrate the explanatory power of theory. With paradox theory, the cases of Ghosn and Johnson offer an opportunity for a narrative explanation that illuminates the dynamics of reversal characteristic of paradox.

6.1.3 Theory to Theory

Another possibility may consist in moving from theory to theory. In this case, a given theory is approached from the perspective of paradox. For example, charismatic leadership (Conger and Kanungo, 1987) may be submitted to the lens of paradox, seeing it as a double-edged sword. A paradox view of charisma illustrates both the promises and the perils of this social process. The charismatic leader attracts followers; the followers augment the charisma with their devotion; the charismatic leader then begins to believe in the power of the hype surrounding them and exceeds their capacities and the limits of their leading. Perhaps one Donald J. Trump could be used as an example here. This application can be used to tap the meta-theoretical power of paradox, using contradiction as an angle to illuminate dimensions of the theory that go unnoticed without the consideration of paradox.

6.2 Applying Paradoxes

This section focusses on how paradox can inform practice. The practical implications of paradox have been analysed. The consequences of ignoring paradox are known; over time, ignorance can result in circularity (namely dangerous vicious circles; see Masuch 1985). It is also known that today's solutions will become tomorrow's problems (Greiner, 1998). There are some illustrative examples, such as Jay (2013), Lüscher and Lewis (2008), and Padavic and colleagues (2020), that used paradox-in-practice to explain its power and shortcoming. Jay (2013), for example, considered the challenge of applying paradox in a hybrid setting and the consequences of ignoring paradox.

In their action research at the Danish company Lego, Lüscher and Lewis (2008) combined sophisticated theorizing with a directed research question to understand the paradoxes with which the hardship of change confronted managers. In this view, managing change consists to some extent in articulating paradoxes. Padavic and colleagues (2020) discuss how interventions can have unintended, surprising effects. In this case, policies aimed at increasing gender equality end up producing more gender inequality. This study offers an important view of the idea of paradox (that is not used deliberately in the text) as absurd, as when something supposed to produce positive effects results in negative consequences. The tension between positive and negative as duality has been acknowledged by positive organizational scholarship authors (e.g., Cameron, 2017; Cunha et al., 2020), who have observed the potential of positivity in negative events, as well as the possible toxicity of positive interventions.

In general, practical applications of paradoxes have been identified, such as analysing polarities (Johnson, 1992), promoting integrative thinking (Martin, 2007), and 'both-and' forms of leadership (Smith et al., 2016). Recent work is articulating paradox theory with management practice in domains such as leadership (Cunha et al., 2021) and innovation (Lewis et al., 2014), informing management practice with paradox theory. Thus, in terms of application, paradox theory has implications to offer. We present examples at different levels of analysis (for a more developed discussion, see Cunha et al., 2021) that researchers can pursue.

6.2.1 Thinking Paradoxically

Organizations may prepare their members to accept the paradoxical condition of organizations. The implementation of paradoxical solutions may benefit from the adoption of a paradox mindset. Actors' 'mindsets encouraged them to value, accept, and feel comfortable with contradictions' (Miron-Spektor et al., 2018: 38). In this case, people may be trained to thrive in the presence of tension and ambiguity. Instead of removing ambiguity or avoiding tension, these may instead be unearthed to support paradoxical sense-making. As Benbenisty and Luria (2021) have explained, different ways of thinking can be activated to use tension – some more promising than others. Using tension to leverage solutions that transcend paradoxes can offer ways of integrating the competing goals that are commonplace in organizational life.

A paradoxical view may be used to recommend caution about excellence, often viewed as a positive state. Yet excellence is a process, impermanent rather than fixed. Organizations may cultivate the notion that it is important to think about ourselves as 'works in progress' in which learning and evolving are more important processes than protecting one's areas of competence at any cost – the attitude Dweck (2008) called a growth mindset. From a paradox perspective, success and excellence contain the seeds of their opposites, namely failure and decay. Therefore, excellence is better viewed with an element of suspicion – as transmitted by the yin-yang.

6.2.2 Teaming Paradoxically

Teams can also be considered paradoxical units crossed by tension and contradiction. To respect teams' paradoxical attributes, it is important to acknowledge those traits. Teams involve a measure of proximity between people but also require inter-member distance – the so-called hedgehog effect (Kets de Vries, 2017). Among other tensions, teams benefit from winning and losing (Silva et al., 2013); they need diversity but may display comfort with homogeneity. For these reasons, organizations may train their people or design them to think/act as paradoxical units. One case from an architectural setting involves artists and/or constructing architects working in what are normally teams of architects and engineers. In terms of involving a constructing architect, they serve as the bridge to focus on interdependence between the two competing camps. Their role is to 'serve as a third person and make sure one side (either poetics or techne) does not dominate the other and that the interdependence between these competing forces is sufficiently exploited. The third person facilitates and makes sure that multiple voices are heard' (Gaim, 2018: 507).

Another avenue to develop teaming through paradox consists in recognizing paradox to mitigate groupthink. Here the paradox logic may also serve to reduce the risk of processes such as groupthink – the pressure for accepting group norms acritically. Groupthink is a process with deleterious consequences, as it cancels the diversity of points of view in favour of consensual unanimity (true or false). Teams can use paradox to counter groupthink processes by using mechanisms such as devil's advocacy. People playing this role introduce an element of tension and highlight the hidden pole, forcing others to think paradoxically. Alternatively, they may use humour, irony and other ways of undercutting and attacking conformity and obedience (Clegg et al., 2021; Jarzabkowski and Lê, 2017).

6.2.3 Organizing Paradoxically

Organizations may also use paradoxes at a more macro level to operationalize the contradictions inherent to the organization. Organizing through paradox might take two routes: cultivating ambidexterity (O'Reilly and Tushman, 2004) and avoiding contradictory rules.

Cultivating ambidexterity constitutes an invitation to think in both-and terms. It is tempting for managers to think in dualistic terms such as planning-improvisation, present-future or profit-progress. A paradox approach constitutes an invitation to embrace a non-dualistic logic. Thinking in terms of both-and means that, in some cases, organizations may find synergies in opposition. Ambidexterity already explains how some of these ideas may be implemented. In the logic of ambidexterity, instead of preferring exploration or exploitation, organizations harmonize both.

Countering contradictory rules. Organizations often accumulate rules that will contradict other rules. For those organizational members impeded from countering them because of their lack of power and agency, these rules may be paralyzing (Berti and Simpson, 2021). For this reason, organizations may conduct sludge audits (Sunstein, 2020) to remove unnecessary administrative noise. This will equip organizational members with the agency for conflicting rules with traits of pragmatic paradoxicality. Instead of confronting people with fixed rules that must be obeyed, organizations may give them a voice to transform rules into a source of coordination rather than in a mechanism of coercion (Adler and Borys, 1996).

While offering paradox as an alternative, we are cognizant that it is not a panacea, a cure for all problems. It is tempting to assume win-win advantages in both-and approaches. Maybe because of novelty, paradox has been approached mainly via its 'bright side', the synergistic potential that leads some authors to assume that other approaches such as 'if-then' reasoning are simplistic in comparison. We advise our readers not to be excessively optimistic about paradox as a cure for organizational ills and about its superiority over the contingency power of 'if-then' thinking.

Paradox can reveal opportunities for synergy but may also fail to deliver its promise. As mounting evidence indicates, managing contradictions involves the knotting and re-knotting of multiple tensions over time (Jarzabkowski et al., 2021a; Sheep et al., 2017), which constitutes a formidable task. Keeping a dynamic tension between opposing forces is difficult and managers often revert to a dominant pole. Danone CEO Emmanuel Faber was pressed to leave, charged with paying excessive attention to the planet over profit (Van Gansbeke, 2021). Apparently, a paradoxical approach did not work for him. Of course, this overemphasis on one pole was not his exclusively, and companies may find it difficult to sustain a balanced integration of goals, as is evident in the case of companies that fell into an impasse after attempts to embrace commercial and sustainability practices (Kok, de Bakker and Groenewegen, 2019) or ended up abandoning paradoxical mindsets in favour of more linear business logic (Sharma and Jaiswal, 2018).

7 Concluding Note

Our work can be read as an invitation to explore paradox as a lens and as a way of informing practice. In a world full of challenges, paradox can offer a stepping stone to make sense of problems such as political polarization, identity, inequality and to question the linear views of organizational functioning. Paradox, however, is no panacea, just a way of thinking afresh about the identification of solutions to complex and competing demands that require collaboration, co-creation and coopetition, among other processes pervaded by contradiction. Paradoxical problems require paradoxical solutions. In a complex world, finding comfort in simplicity may be tempting, but it is not more than a comfortable illusion. The message of paradox enters here: let us not treat complex processes as if they were simple, and a measure of simplicity is necessary to keep the world manageable. The question is: how much simplicity can be used to explain a complex world?

References

Abdallah, C., Denis, J.-L. and Langley, A. (2011). Having your cake and eating it too: Discourses of transcendence and their role in organizational change dynamics. *Journal of Organizational Change Management* 24(3): 333–48.

Abrantes, A., Cunha, M. P. and Miner, A. S. (2021). *Elgar introduction to organizational improvisation*. Cheltenham: Edward Elgar.

Achtenhagen, L., and Melin L. (2003). Managing the homogeneity-heterogeneity duality. In A. Pettigrew, R. Whittington, L. Melin et al. (eds.), *Innovative forms of organizing* (pp. 301–27). London: Sage.

Adler, P. S., and Borys, B. (1996). Two types of bureaucracy: Enabling and coercive. *Administrative Science Quarterly* 41(1): 61–89.

Adler, P. S., Goldoftas, B. and Levine, D. I. (1999). Flexibility versus efficiency? A case study of model changeovers in the Toyota production system. *Organization Science* 10(1): 43–68.

Alvesson, M., and Kärreman, D. (2000). Varieties of discourse: On the study of organizations through discourse analysis. *Human Relations* 53: 1125–49.

Andriopoulos, C., and Lewis, M. W. (2009). Exploitation-exploration tensions and organizational ambidexterity: Managing paradoxes of innovation. *Organization Science* 20(4): 696–717.

Andriopoulos, C., and Lewis, M. W. (2010). Managing innovation paradoxes: Ambidexterity lessons from leading product design companies. *Long Range Planning* 43(1): 104–22.

Aoki, K., and Wilhelm, M. (2017). The role of ambidexterity in managing buyer-supplier relationships: The Toyota case. *Organization Science* 28(6): 1080–97.

Ashforth, B. E. (1991). The whys and wherefores of organizational Catch-22s: Common types and their implications for organization development. *Public Administration Quarterly* 14(4): 457–82.

Ashforth, B. E., and Reingen, P. H. (2014). Functions of dysfunction: Managing the dynamics of an organizational duality in a natural food cooperative. *Administrative Science Quarterly* 59(3): 474–516.

Ashforth, B. E., Rogers, K. M., Pratt, M. G. and Pradies, C. (2014). Ambivalence in organizations: A multilevel approach. *Organization Science* 25(5): 1453–78. https://doi.org/10.1287/orsc.2014.0909.

Bansal. P. (2017). *Monsanto Company: Doing business in India*, by Robert D. Klassen. *Academy of Management Learning & Education* 16(3): 484–5.

Bansal, P., Kim, A. and Wood, M. O. (2018). Hidden in plain sight: The importance of scale in organizations' attention to issues. *Academy of Management Review* 43(2): 217–41.

Bartunek, J. M. (1988). The dynamics of personal and organizational reframing. In R. Quinn and K. Cameron (eds.), *Paradox and transformation: Towards a theory of change in organization and management* (pp. 137–62). Cambridge, MA: Ballinger.

Battilana, J., and Dorado, S. (2010). Building sustainable hybrid organizations: The case of commercial microfinance organizations. *Academy of Management Journal* 53(6): 1419–40.

Baxter, J., Hewitt, B. and Haynes, M. (2008). Life course transitions and housework: Marriage, parenthood, and time on housework. *Journal of Marriage and Family* 70(2): 259–72.

Beck, S., and Ogden, T. (2007). Beware of bad microcredit. *Harvard Business Review* 85(9): 20–2.

Bednarek, R., Cunha, M. P., Schad, J. et al. (2021a). The value of interdisciplinary research to advance paradox in organization theory. In R. Bednarek, M. P. Cunha, J. Schad and W. K. Smith (eds.), *Interdisciplinary dialogues on organizational paradox: Learning from belief and science, Part A* (pp. 3–25). Bingley, UK: Emerald.

Bednarek, R., Cunha, M. P., Schad, J. et al. (2021b). Implementing interdisciplinary paradox research. In R. Bednarek, M. P. Cunha, J. Schad et al. (eds.), *Interdisciplinary dialogues on organizational paradox: Investigating social structures and human expression, Part B* (pp. 3–24). Bingley, UK: Emerald.

Beech, N., Burns, H., Caestecker, L. D., MacIntosh, R. and Maclean, D. (2004). Paradox as invitation to act in problematic change situations. *Human Relations* 57(10): 1313–32.

Benbenisty, Y., and Luria, G. (2021). A time to act and a time for restraint: Everyday sensegiving in the context of paradox. *Journal of Organizational Behavior* 42(8): 1005–22.

Benson, J. K. (1977). Organizations: A dialectical view. *Administrative Science Quarterly* 22: 1–21.

Berger, P., and Luckmann, T. (1966). *The social construction of reality: A treatise in the sociology of knowledge.* Garden City, NJ: Doubleday.

Berger, P., and Pullberg, S. (1966). Reification and the sociological critique of consciousness. *New Left Review* (35): 56–71.

Bernerth, J. B., Walker, H. J. and Harris, S. G. (2011). Change fatigue: Development and initial validation of a new measure. *Work and Stress* 25(4): 321–37.

Berti, M. (2017). *Elgar introduction to organizational discourse analysis.* Cheltenham: Edward Elgar.

Berti, M. (2021). Logic(s) and paradox. In R. Bednarek, M. P. Cunha, J. Schad et al. (eds.), *Interdisciplinary dialogues on organizational paradox: Investigating social structures and human expression* (pp. 27–47). Bingley, UK: Emerald.

Berti, M., and Simpson, A. V. (2021). The dark side of organizational paradoxes: The dynamics of disempowerment. *Academy of Management Review* 46(2): 252–74.

Berti, M., Simpson, A. V., Cunha, M. P. and Clegg. S. (2021). *Elgar introduction to organizational paradox theory.* Cheltenham: Edward Elgar.

Besharov, M. L., and Smith, W. K. (2014). Multiple institutional logics in organizations: Explaining their varied nature and implications. *Academy of Management Review* 39(3): 364–81.

Bhaskar, R. (1977). *A realist theory of science.* London: Verso.

Boldizzoni, F. (2020). *Foretelling the end of capitalism: Intellectual misadventures since Karl Marx.* Cambridge, MA: Harvard University Press.

Boulding, K. E. (1956). General systems theory: The skeleton of science. *Management Science* 2(3): 197–208.

Brix-Asala, C., Geisbüsch, A. K., Sauer, P. C., Schöpflin, P. and Zehendner, A. (2018). Sustainability tensions in supply chains: A case study of paradoxes and their management. *Sustainability* 10(2): 1–20.

Brown, S. L., and Eisenhardt, K. M. (1997). The art of continuous change: Linking complexity theory and time-paced evolution in relentlessly shifting organizations. *Administrative Science Quarterly* 42(1): 1–34.

Bucknell, K. (2000). Who is Christopher Isherwood? In J. J. Berg and C. Freeman (eds.), *The Isherwood century: Essays in the life and works of Christopher Isherwood* (pp. 13–29). Madison: University of Wisconsin Press.

Busse, C., Kach, A. P. and Wagner, S. M. (2017). Boundary conditions: What they are, how to explore them, why we need them, and when to consider them. *Organizational Research Methods* 20(4): 574–609.

Bygdås, A. L., Clegg, S. R. and Hagen, A. L. (2019). *Media management and digital transformation.* London: Routledge.

Byggeth, S., and Hochschorner, E. (2006). Handling trade-offs in ecodesign tools for sustainable product development and procurement. *Journal of Cleaner Production* 14(15–16): 1420–30.

Cameron, K. S. (2017). Paradox in positive organizational scholarship.In W. K. Smith, M. Lewis, P. Jarzabkowski and A. Langley (eds.), *The Oxford handbook of organizational paradoxes* (pp. 216–38). Oxford: Oxford University Press.

Cameron, K. S., and Quinn, R. E. (1988). *Paradox and transformation: Toward a theory of change in organization and management*. Cambridge, MA: Ballinger.

Carollo, L., and Guerci, M. (2018). 'Activists in a suit': Paradoxes and metaphors in sustainability managers' identity work. *Journal of Business Ethics* 148(2): 249–68.

Carton, A. M. (2018). 'I'm not mopping the floors, I'm putting a man on the moon': How NASA leaders enhanced the meaningfulness of work by changing the meaning of work. *Administrative Science Quarterly* 63(2): 323–69.

Castilla, E. J., and Benard, S. (2010). The paradox of meritocracy in organizations. *Administrative Science Quarterly* 55(4): 543–676.

Chen, M.-J. (2002). Transcending paradox: The Chinese 'middle way' perspective. *Asia Pacific Journal of Management* 19(2): 179–99.

Chen, M.-J. (2008). Reconceptualizing the competition-cooperation relationship: A transparadox perspective. *Journal of Management Inquiry* 17(4): 288–304.

Clegg, S. R. (2002). General introduction. In S. R. Clegg (ed.), *Management and organization paradoxes* (pp. 1–10). Amsterdam:John Benjamins.

Clegg, S. R., Cunha, J. V. and Cunha, M. P. (2002). Management paradoxes: A relational view. *Human Relations* 55(5): 483–503.

Clegg, S. R., and Cunha, M. P. (2017). Organizational dialectics. In W. K. Smith, M. W. Lewis, P. Jarzabkowski, et al. (eds.), *The Oxford handbook of organizational paradox* (pp. 105–24). Oxford: Oxford University Press.

Clegg, S. R., Cunha, M. P. and Berti, M. (2022). Research movements and theorizing dynamics in management and organization studies. *Academy of Management Review* 47(3):382–401.

Clegg, S. R., Cunha, M. P., Munro, I. et al. (2016). Kafkaesque power and bureaucracy. *Journal of Political Power* 9(2): 157–81.

Clegg, S., Cunha, M. P., Rego, A. and Berti, M. (2021). The academic as jester stimulating management learning. *Management Learning*.

Clegg, S. R., Kornberger, M. and Rhodes, C. (2005). Learning/becoming/organizing. *Organization* 12: 147–67.

Coget, J. F., and Keller, E. (2010). The critical decision vortex: Lessons from the emergency room. *Journal of Management Inquiry* 19(1): 56–67.

Collins, D. (1994). The disempowering logic of empowerment. *Empowerment in Organizations* 2(2): 14–21.

Conger, J. A., and Kanungo, R. N. (1987). Toward a behavioral theory of charismatic leadership in organizational settings. *Academy of Management Review* 12(4): 637–47.

Cunha, J. V., Clegg, S. R. and Cunha, M. P. (2002). Management, paradox, and permanent dialectics. In S. R. Clegg (ed.), *Management and organization paradoxes* (pp. 1–10). Philadelphia, PA: John Benjamins.

Cunha, M. P., Clegg, S. R., Rego, A. et al. (2021). *Paradoxes of power and leadership*. Abingdon: Routledge.

Cunha, M. P., Fortes, A., Gomes, E. et al. (2019b). Ambidextrous leadership, paradox and contingency: Evidence from Angola. *International Journal of Human Resource Management* 30(4): 702–27.

Cunha, M. P., Giustiniano, L., Rego, A. et al. (2017). Mission impossible? The paradoxes of stretch goal setting. *Management Learning* 48(2): 40–57.

Cunha, M. P., Kamoche, K. and Cunha, R. C. (2003). Organizational improvisation and leadership: A field study in two computer-mediated settings. *International Studies of Management & Organization* 33(1): 34–57.

Cunha, M. P., Neves, P., Clegg, S., Costa, S. and Rego, A. (2019). Paradoxes of organizational change in a merger context. *Qualitative Research in Organizations and Management: An International Journal* 14(3): 217–40.

Cunha, M. P., and Putnam, L. L. (2019). Paradox theory and the paradox of success. *Strategic Organization* 17(1): 95–106.

Cunha, M. P., Rego, A., Simpson. A. and Clegg, S. (2020). *Positive organizational behavior: A reflective approach*. London: Routledge.

Cunha, M. P., Simpson, A. V., Clegg, S. R. et al. (2019a). Speak! Paradoxical effects of a managerial culture of 'speaking up'. *British Journal of Management* 30(4): 829–46.

Cunha, M. P., Simpson, A. V., Rego, A. and Clegg, S. (2022). Non-naïve organizational positivity through a generative paradox pedagogy. *Management Learning* 53(1): 15–32.

Cunha, M. P., Zoogah, D., Wood, G. et al. (2020). Guest editorial. *Journal of Knowledge Management* 24(1): 1–7.

Cuonzo, M. (2014). *Paradox*. Cambridge, MA: MIT Press.

Cuonzo, M. (2022). The power of paradoxes. *New Scientist* 253(3368): 44–8.

Da Silveira, G., and Slack, N. (2001). Exploring the trade-off concept. *International Journal of Operations and Production Management* 21(7): 949–64.

Daston, L. (2014). Wonder and the ends of inquiry. *Point Magazine*, 11 June. https://thepointmag.com/examined-life/wonder-ends-inquiry/. Accessed 17 August 2021.

Denison, D. R., Hooijberg, R. and Quinn, R. E. (1995). Paradox and performance: Toward a theory of behavioral complexity in managerial leadership. *Organization Science* 6(5): 524–40.

Donaldson, L. (1987). Strategy and structural adjustment to regain fit and performance: In defence of contingency theory. *Journal of Management Studies* 24(1): 1–24.

Dunbar, R. L., and Garud, R. (2009). Distributed knowledge and indeterminate meaning: The case of the *Columbia* shuttle flight. *Organization Studies* 30(4): 397–421.

Dweck, C. S. (2008). Can personality be changed? The role of beliefs in personality and change. *Current Directions in Psychological Science* 17(6): 391–4.

Eden, C., Jones, S., Sims, D. et al. (1981). The intersubjectivity of issues and issues of intersubjectivity. *Journal of Management Studies* 18(1): 37–47.

Edgecliffe-Johnson, A., Hill, A. and Kuchler, H. (2021). Is McKinsey losing its mystique? *Financial Times*, 23 February, 17.

Engeström, Y., and Sannino, A. (2011). Discursive manifestations of contradictions in organizational change efforts: A methodological framework. *Journal of Organizational Change Management* 24(3): 368–87.

Fairhurst, G. T., and Grant, D. (2010). The social construction of leadership: A sailing guide. *Management Communication Quarterly* 24(2): 171–210.

Fairhurst, G. T., and Putnam, L. L. (2019). An integrative methodology for organizational oppositions: Aligning grounded theory and discourse analysis. *Organizational Research Methods* 22(4): 917–40.

Farjoun, M. (2010). Beyond dualism: Stability and change as a duality. *Academy of Management Review* 35(2): 202–25.

Farjoun, M. (2016). Contradictions, dialectics. In A. Langley and H. Tsoukas (eds.), *The Sage handbook of process organization studies* (pp. 87–109). London: Sage.

Farjoun, M. (2019). Strategy and dialectics: Rejuvenating a long-standing relationship. *Strategic Organization* 17(1): 133–44.

Farjoun, M. (2021). The becoming of change in 3D: Dialectics, Darwin and Dewey. In M. S. Poole and A. Van de Ven (eds.), *The Oxford handbook of organizational change and innovation* (2nd ed.). New York: Oxford University Press. https://doi.org/10.1093/oxfordhb/9780198845973.013.38.

Farjoun, M., Ansell, C. and Boin, A. (2015). PERSPECTIVE: Pragmatism in organization studies: Meeting the challenges of a dynamic and complex world. *Organization Science* 26(6): 1787–1804.

Ferguson, K. E. (1984).*The feminist case against bureaucracy*. Temple, IN: Temple University Press.

Festinger, L. (1957). *A theory of cognitive dissonance*. Stanford, CA: Stanford University Press.

Ford, J. D., and Ford, L. W. (1994), Logics of identity, contradiction, and attraction in change. *Academy of Management Review* 19(4): 756–85.

Francis, H., and Keegan, A. (2020). The ethics of engagement in an age of austerity: A paradox perspective. *Journal of Business Ethics* 162(3): 593–607.

Gaim, M. (2017). *Paradox as the new normal: Essays on framing, managing and sustaining organizational tensions*. Umeå: Umeå University.

Gaim, M. (2018). On the emergence and management of paradoxical tensions: The case of architectural firms. *European Management Journal* 36(4): 497–518.

Gaim, M., and Clegg, S. R. (2021). Paradox beyond East/West orthodoxy: The case of Ubuntu. In R. Bednarek, M. P. Cunha, J. Schad et al. (eds.), *Interdisciplinary dialogues on organizational paradox: Investigating social structures and human expression. Part A* (Research in the Sociology of Organizations, Vol. 73a) (pp. 29–50). Bingley, UK: Emerald.

Gaim, M., Clegg, S. and Cunha, M. P. (2021). Managing impressions rather than emissions: Volkswagen and the false mastery of paradox. *Organization Studies* 42(6): 949–70.

Gaim, M., Clegg, S. and Cunha, M. P. (2022). In praise of paradox persistence: Evidence from the Sydney Opera House Project. *Project Management Journal* 53(4): 397–415.

Gaim, M., and Wåhlin, N. (2016). In search of a creative space: A conceptual framework of synthesizing paradoxical tensions. *Scandinavian Journal of Management* 32(1): 33–44.

Gaim, M., Wåhlin, N., Cunha M. P. et al. (2018) Analyzing competing demands in organizations: A systematic comparison. *Journal of Organization Design* 7(1): 1–16.

Garland T., Jr. (2014). Trade-offs. *Current Biology* 24(2): R60–R61.

Geppert, M., and Williams, K. (2006). Global, national and local practices in multinational corporations: Towards a sociopolitical framework. *International Journal of Human Resource Management* 17(1): 49–69.

Goffman, E. (1956). *The presentation of self in everyday life*. Harmondsworth: Penguin.

Goffman, E. (1974). *Frame analysis: An essay on the organization of experience*. Cambridge, MA: Harvard University Press.

Gotsi, M., Andriopoulos, C., Lewis, M. W. et al. (2010). Managing creatives: Paradoxical approaches to identity regulation. *Human Relations* 63(6): 781–805.

Greiner, L. E. (1998). Evolution and revolution as organizations grow. *Harvard Business Review* 76(3): 55–64.

Gümüsay, A. A., Smets, M. and Morris, T. (2020). 'God at work': Engaging central and incompatible institutional logics through elastic hybridity. *Academy of Management Journal* 63(1): 124–54.

Hage, G. (2009). Waiting out the crisis: On stuckedness and governmentality. *Anthropological Theory* 5: 463–75.

Hahn, T., Figge, F., Pinkse, J. et al. (2018). A paradox perspective on corporate sustainability: Descriptive, instrumental, and normative aspects. *Journal of Business Ethics* 148(2): 235–48.

Hahn, T., and Knight, E. (2021). The ontology of organizational paradox: A quantum approach. *Academy of Management Review* 46(2): 362–84.

Hahn, T., Preuss, L., Pinkse, J. et al. (2015). Cognitive frames in corporate sustainability: Managerial sensemaking with paradoxical and business case frames. *Academy of Management Review* 4015: 18–42.

Hallyday, F. (1996). A Cold War tragedy in Afghanistan that the world forgot. *Irish Times.* 11 May. www.irishtimes.com/news/a-cold-war-tragedy-in-afghanistan-that-the-world-forgot-1.48054. Accessed 17 August 2021.

Hargrave, T. J. (2020). The paradox perspective and the dialectics of contradictions research. In M. S. Poole and A. H. Van de Ven (eds.), *The Oxford handbook of organizational change and innovation* (pp. 161–85). Oxford: Oxford University Press.

Hargrave, T. J., and Van de Ven, A. H. (2017). Integrating dialectical and paradox perspectives on managing contradictions in organizations. *Organization Studies* 38(3–4): 319–39.

Harvey, J. B. (1988). The Abilene paradox: The management of agreement. *Organizational Dynamics* 17(1): 17–43.

Hengst, I.-A., Jarzabkowski, P., Hoegl, M. et al. (2019). Toward a process theory of making sustainability strategies legitimate in action. *Academy of Management Journal.* https://doi.org/10.5465/amj.2016.0960.

Hernes, T., and Bakken, T. (2003). Implications of self-reference: Niklas Luhmann's autopoiesis and organization theory. *Organization Studies* 24(9): 1511–35.

Huq, J.-L., Reay, T. and Chreim, S. 2017. Protecting the paradox of interprofessional collaboration. *Organization Studies* 38(3–4): 513–38.

Hussain, N., Rigoni, U. and Orij, R. P. (2018). Corporate governance and sustainability performance: Analysis of triple bottom line performance. *Journal of Business Ethics* 149(2): 411–32.

Husserl, E. (1965 [1935]). *The crisis of European sciences and transcendental phenomenology: An introduction to phenomenological philosophy.* New York: Harper and Row.

Iivonen, K. (2018). Defensive responses to strategic sustainability paradoxes: Have your Coke and drink it too! *Journal of Business Ethics* 148(2): 309–27.

Isherwood, C. (1954). *Goodbye to Berlin*. London: Hogarth.

Janssens, M., and Steyaert, C. (1999). The world in two and a third way out? The concept of duality in organization theory and practice. *Scandinavian Journal of Management* 15(2): 121–39.

Jarzabkowski, P., Bednarek, R., Chalkias, C. and Cacciatori, E. (2021a). Enabling rapid financial response to disasters: Knotting and reknotting multiple paradoxes in interorganizational systems. *Academy of Management Journal*.

Jarzabkowski, P., Bednarek, R., Kilminster, W. et al. (2021b). An integrative approach to investigating longstanding organisational phenomena: Opportunities for practice theorists and historians. *Business History* 1–9.

Jarzabkowski, P., and Lê, J. K. (2017). We have to do this and that? You must be joking: Constructing and responding to paradox through humor. *Organization Studies* 38(3–4): 433–62.

Jarzabkowski, P., Lê, J. K. and Van de Ven, A. H. (2013). Responding to competing strategic demands: How organizing, belonging, and performing paradoxes coevolve. *Strategic Organization* 11(3): 245–80.

Jay. J. (2013). Navigating paradox as a mechanism of change and innovation in hybrid organizations. *Academy of Management Journal* 56(1): 137–59.

Jenkins, S. (2021). It has taken 20 years to prove the invasion of Afghanistan was totally unnecessary. *The Guardian*. 16 August. www.theguardian.com/commentisfree/2021/aug/16/20-years-invasion-afghanistan-unnecessary-post-imperial-fantasy. Accessed 17 August 2021.

Johnson, B. (1992). *Polarity management: Identifying and managing unsolvable problems*. Middleville, MI: Human Resource Development.

Joseph, J., Borland, H., Orlitzky, M. and Lindgreen, A. (2020). Seeing versus doing: How businesses manage tensions in pursuit of sustainability. *Journal of Business Ethics* 164(2): 349–70.

Kanter, R. M. (2008). *Men and women of the corporation*. New York: Basic Books.

Katz, D., and Kahn, R. (1978). *The social psychology of organizations*. New York: Wiley.

Keller, J., Loewenstein, J. and Yan, J. (2017). Culture, conditions and paradoxical frames. *Organization Studies* 38(3–4): 539–60.

Keller, J., Wen Chen, E. and Leung, A. K.-Y. (2018). How national culture influences individuals' subjective experience with paradoxical tensions. *Cross Cultural and Strategic Management* 25(3): 443–67.

Keller, J., Wong, S.-S. and Liou, S. (2020). How social networks facilitate collective responses to organizational paradoxes. *Human Relations* 73(3): 401–28.

Kets de Vries, M. F. R. (2017). *Riding the leadership rollercoaster.* Cham, Switzerland: Springer.

Kiefhaber, E., Pavlovich, K. and Spraul, K. (2020). Sustainability-related identities and the institutional environment: The case of New Zealand: Owners–managers of small- and medium-sized hospitality businesses. *Journal of Business Ethics* 163(1): 37–51.

King, A. A., and Pucker, K. P. (2021). The dangerous allure of win-win strategies. *Stanford Social Innovation Review* Winter: 35–9.

Knight, E., and Paroutis, S. (2017). Becoming salient: The TMT leader's role in shaping the interpretive context of paradoxical tensions. *Organization Studies* 38(3–4): 403–32.

Kok, A. M., de Bakker, F. G. and Groenewegen, P. (2019). Sustainability struggles: Conflicting cultures and incompatible logics. *Business and Society* 58(8): 1496–1532.

Lalaounis, S. T., and Nayak, A. (2021). Dynamic stability: Unfolding dynamics of vicious cycles in a design firm. *European Management Journal* 40(1): 137–50.

Langley, A., Smallman, C., Tsoukas, H. et al. (2013). Process studies of change in organization and management: Unveiling temporality, activity, and flow. *Academy of Management Journal* 56(1): 1–13.

Lawrence, P. R., and Lorsch, J. W. (1967). Differentiation and integration in complex organizations. *Administrative Science Quarterly* 12(1): 1–47.

Le Guin, U. K. (2011). Lao Tzu: Tao Te Ching: A book about the way and the power of the way. Shambhala Publications.

Leonard-Barton, D. (1992). Core capabilities and core rigidities: A paradox in managing new product development. *Strategic Management Journal* 13(S1): 111–25.

Levinson, H. M. (1960). Pattern bargaining: A case study of the automobile workers. *Quarterly Journal of Economics* 74(2): 296–317.

Lewis, M. W. (2000). Exploring paradox: Toward a more comprehensive guide. *Academy of Management Review* 25(4): 760–76.

Lewis, M. W., Andriopoulos, C. and Smith, W. K. (2014). Paradoxical leadership to enable strategic agility. *California Management Review* 56(3): 58–77.

Lewis, M. W., and Dehler, G. E. (2000). Learning through paradox: A pedagogical strategy for exploring contradictions and complexity. *Journal of Management Education* 24(6): 708–25.

Lewis, M. W., and Smith, W. K. (2014). Paradox as a metatheoretical perspective: Sharpening the focus and widening the scope. *Journal of Applied Behavioral Science* 50(2): 127–49.

Li, P. P. (1998). Towards a geocentric framework of organizational form: A holistic, dynamic and paradoxical approach. *Organization Studies* 19(5): 829–61.

Li, P. P. (2016). Global implications of the indigenous epistemological system from the East: How to apply yin-yang balancing to paradox management. *Cross Cultural and Strategic Management* 23(1): 42–77.

Li, X. (2014). Can yin-yang guide Chinese indigenous management research? *Management and Organization Review* 10(1): 7–27.

Li, X. (2021). Solving paradox by reducing expectation. *Academy of Management Review* 46(2): 406–8.

Lindberg, O., Rantatalo, O. and Hällgren, M. (2017). Making sense through false syntheses: Working with paradoxes in the reorganization of the Swedish police. *Scandinavian Journal of Management* 33(3): 175–84.

Lindsay, R. M., and Libby, T. (2007). Svenska Handelsbanken: Controlling a radically decentralized organization without budgets. *Issues in Accounting Education* 22(4): 625–40.

Luhmann, N. (1995). *Social systems*. Stanford, CA: Stanford University Press.

Luhmann, N. (2018). *Organization and decision*. Cambridge: Cambridge University Press.

Lüscher, L. S., and Lewis, M. W. (2008). Organizational change and managerial sensemaking: Working through paradox. *Academy of Management Journal* 51(2): 221–40.

Maclean, M., Harvey, C., Golant, B. D. and Sillince, J. A. (2020). The role of innovation narratives in accomplishing organizational ambidexterity. *Strategic Organization* 19(4): 693–721.

Manzhynski, S. (2021). Understanding and managing coopetition for sustainability: Process and outcomes (Doctoral dissertation, Umeå University).

March, J. G. (1991). Exploration and exploitation in organizational learning. *Organization Science* 26(3): 327–42.

March, J. G. (2010). *The ambiguities of experience*. Cornell, NY: Cornell University Press.

Marti, E., and Gond, J.-P. (2018). When do theories become self-fulfilling? Exploring the boundary conditions of performativity. *Academy of Management Review* 43(3): 487–508.

Martin, R. (2007). *The opposable mind: How successful leaders win through integrative thinking*. Boston, MA: Harvard Business School Press.

Martin, R. (2009). *The design of business: Why design thinking is the next competitive advantage*. Boston, MA: Harvard Business School Press.

Marx, K. (1976). *Capital*. London: NLR Books/Penguin.

Masuch, M. (1985). Vicious circles in organizations. *Administrative Science Quarterly* 30(1): 14–33.

McCall, L. (2005). The complexity of intersectionality. *Signs: Journal of Women in Culture and Society* 30(3): 1771–1800.

Merton, R. K. (1936). The unanticipated consequences of purposive social action. *American Sociological Review* 1(6): 894–904.

Metcalf, W. (1940). The reality of the unobservable. *Philosophy of Science* 7(3): 337–41.

Meyer, E. (2014). *The culture map: Breaking through the invisible boundaries of global business*. Amsterdam: Public Affairs.

Miller, D. (1992). The Icarus paradox: How exceptional companies bring about their own downfall. *Business Horizons* 35(1): 24–35.

Mills, C. W. (2000). *The sociological imagination*. Oxford: Oxford University Press.

Miron-Spektor, E., Erez, M. and Naveh, E. (2011a). The effect of conformist and attentive-to-detail members on team innovation: Reconciling the innovation paradox. *Academy of Management Journal* 54(4): 740–60.

Miron-Spektor, E., Gino, F. and Argote, L. (2011b). Paradoxical frames and creative sparks: Enhancing individual creativity through conflict and integration. *Organizational Behavior and Human Decision Processes* 116(2): 229–40.

Miron-Spektor, E., Ingram, A., Keller, J., Smith, W. and Lewis, M. (2018). Microfoundations of organizational paradox: The problem is how we think about the problem. *Academy of Management Journal* 61(1): 26–45.

Murnighan, J. K., and Conlon, D. E. (1991). The dynamics of intense work groups: A study of British string quartets. *Administrative Science Quarterly* 36(2): 165–86.

Nayak, A. (2016). Wisdom and the tragic question: Moral learning and emotional perception in leadership and organisations. *Journal of Business Ethics* 137(1): 1–13.

Nonaka, I., and Takeuchi, H. (2021). Humanizing strategy. *Long Range Planning*. 102070.

Oakley, J. G. (2000). Gender-based barriers to senior management positions: Understanding the scarcity of female CEOs. *Journal of Business Ethics* 27(4): 321–34.

O'Byrne, D. (2020). Power without responsibility: Populism, narcisism and the contradictions of contemporary capitalism. *International Critical Thought* (10)3: 440–53.

O'Reilly, C. A., and Tushman, M. L. (2004). The ambidextrous organization. *Harvard Business Review* 82(4): 74–81, 140.

O'Reilly, C. A., and Tushman, M. L. (2008). Ambidexterity as a dynamic capability: Resolving the innovator's dilemma. *Research in Organizational Behavior* 28(4): 185–206.

Padavic, I., Ely, R. J. and Reid, E. M. (2020). Explaining the persistence of gender inequality: The work-family narrative as a social defense against the 24/7 work culture. *Administrative Science Quarterly* 65(1): 61–111.

Pamphile, V. D. (2021). Paradox peers: A relational approach to navigating a business-society paradox. *Academy of Management Journal*. https://doi.org/10.5465/amj.2019.0616.

Patrick, H. (2018). Nested tensions and smoothing tactics: An ethnographic examination of ambidexterity in a theatre. *Management Learning* 49(5): 559–77.

Peng, K., and Nisbett, R. E. (1999). Culture, dialectics, and reasoning about contradiction. *American Psychologist* 54(9): 741–54.

Poole, M. S., and Van de Ven, A. H. (1989). Using paradox to build management and organization theories. *Academy of Management Review* 14(4): 562–78.

Popper, K. (2012). *The open society and its enemies*. London: Routledge.

Pradies, C., Carmine, S., Cheal, J. et al. (2021). The lived experience of paradox: How individuals navigate tensions during the pandemic crisis. *Journal of Management Inquiry* 30(2): 154–67.

Pradies, C., Tunarosa, A., Lewis, M. W. et al. (2020). From vicious to virtuous paradox dynamics: The social-symbolic work of supporting actors. *Organization Studies*. https://doi.org/10.1177/0170840620907200.

Prange, C. (2021). Agility as the discovery of slowness. *California Management Review* 63(4): 27–51.

Preuss, L., Pinkse, J., Hahn, T. and Figge, F. (2021). Travelled roads and novel vistas: Taking Stock of empirical studies into tensions in business sustainability. In T. Maak, N. Pless, M. Orlitzky and S. Sandhu (eds.), *The Routledge companion to corporate social responsibility* (pp. 342–54). London: Routledge.

Putnam, L. L., Fairhurst, G. T. and Banghart, S. (2016). Contradictions, dialectics, and paradoxes in organizations: A constitutive approach. *Academy of Management Annals* 10(1): 65–171.

Raffaelli, R., DeJordy, R. and McDonald, R. M. (2021). How leaders with divergent visions generate novel strategy: Navigating the paradox of preservation and modernization in Swiss watchmaking. *Academy of Management Journal*.

Raisch, S., Hargrave, T. J. andVan De Ven, A. H. (2018). The learning spiral: A process perspective on paradox. *Journal of Management Studies* 55(8): 1507–26.

Repenning, N. P., and Sterman, J. D. (2001). Nobody ever gets credit for fixing problems that never happened: Creating and sustaining process improvement. *California Management Review* 43(4): 64–88.

Rhee, M., and Kim, T. (2015). Great vessels take a long time to mature: Early success traps and competences in exploitation and exploration. *Organization Science* 26(1): 180–97.

Ritzer, G. (1990). Metatheorizing in sociology: The basic parameters and the potential contributions of postmodernism. *Sociological Forum* 5(1): 3–15.

Robinson, J. A., and Acemoglu, D. (2012). *Why nations fail: The origins of power, prosperity and poverty.* London: Profile.

Rosales, V. et al. (2022). The rubber band effect: Managing the stability-change paradox in routines. *Scandinavian Journal of Management.*

Rossi, M., Nandhakumar, J. and Mattila, M. (2020). Balancing fluid and cemented routines in a digital workplace. *Journal of Strategic Information Systems* 29(2): 101616.

Sacks, H. (1972). On the analyzability of stories by children'in J.J. Gumperz and D. Hymes (eds.): *Directions in Sociolinguistics: The Ethnography of Communication.* New York: Holt, Rinehart and Winston.

Sandberg, J., & Tsoukas, H. (2015). Making sense of the sensemaking perspective: Its constituents, limitations, and opportunities for further development. *Journal of organizational behavior, 36*(S1), S6–S32.

Schad, J. (2017). Ad fontes: Philosophical foundations of paradox research. In W. K. Smith, M. W. Lewis, P. Jarzabkowski et al. (eds.), *The Oxford handbook of organizational paradox* (pp. 27–47).Oxford: Oxford University Press.

Schad, J., and Bansal, P. (2018). Seeing the forest and the trees: How a systems perspective informs paradox research. *Journal of Management Studies* 55(8): 1490–1506.

Schad, J., Lewis, M. W., Raisch, S. et al. (2016). Paradox research in management science: Looking back to move forward. *Academy of Management Annals* 10(1): 5–64.

Schrage, S., and Rasche, A. (2021). Inter-organizational paradox management: How national business systems affect responses to paradox along a global value chain. *Organization Studies*43(4): 547–71.

Schutz, A. (1967). *The phenomenology of the social world.* Evanston, IL: Northwestern University Press.

Sharma, G., and Bansal, P. (2017). Partners for good: How business and NGOs engage the commercial-social paradox. *Organization Studies* 38(3–4): 341–64.

Sharma, G., and Jaiswal, A. K. (2018). Unsustainability of sustainability: Cognitive frames and tensions in bottom of the pyramid projects. *Journal of Business Ethics* 148(2): 291–307.

Sheep, M. L., Fairhurst, G. T. and Khazanchi, S. (2017). Knots in the discourse of innovation: Investigating multiple tensions in a reacquired spin-off. *Organization Studies* 38(3–4): 463–88.

Silva T., Cunha, M. P., Clegg, S. R. et al. (2013). Smells like team spirit: Opening a paradoxical black box. *Human Relations* 67(3): 287–310.

Simon, H. A. (1996). *The sciences of the artificial.* Cambridge, MA: MIT Press.

Sitkin, S. B., See, K. E., Miller, C. C. et al. (2011). The paradox of stretch goals: Organizations in pursuit of the seemingly impossible. *Academy of Management Review* 36(3): 544–66.

Slawinski, N., and Bansal, P. (2015). Short on time: Intertemporal tensions in business sustainability.*Organization Science* 26(2): 531–49.

Sleesman, D. J. (2019). Pushing through the tension while stuck in the mud: Paradox mindset and escalation of commitment. *Organizational Behavior and Human Decision Processes* 155: 83–96.

Smith, K., and Berg, D. (1987). *Paradoxes of group life: Understanding conflict, paralysis, and movement in group dynamics.* San Francisco, CA: Jossey-Bass.

Smith, W., and Lewis, M. (2011). Towards a theory of paradox: A dynamic equilibrium model of organizing. *Academy of Management Review* 36(2): 381–403.

Smith, W., Lewis, M., and Tushman, M. (2016). Both/and leadership. *Harvard Business Review* 94(5): 62–70.

Smith, W. K. (2014). Dynamic decision making: A model of senior leaders managing strategic paradoxes. *Academy of Management Journal* 57(6): 1592–1623.

Smith, W. K., and Besharov, M. L. (2019). Bowing before dual gods: How structured flexibility sustains organizational hybridity. *Administrative Science Quarterly* 64(1): 1–44.

Smith, W. K., and Cunha, M. P. (2020). A paradoxical approach to hybridity: Integrating dynamic equilibrium and disequilibrium perspectives. *Organizational hybridity: Perspectives, processes, promises.* Bingley, UK: Emerald.

Smith, W. K., Erez, M., Jarvenpaa, S. et al. (2017a). Adding complexity to theories of paradox, tensions, and dualities of innovation and change: Introduction to *Organization Studies* special issue on paradox, tensions, and dualities of innovation and change. *Organization Studies* 38(3–4): 303–17.

Smith, W. K., Lewis, M. W., Jarzabkowski, P. and Langley, A. (eds.) (2017b). *The Oxford handbook of organizational paradox.* Oxford: Oxford University Press.

Smith, W. K., Lewis, M. W., Jarzabkowski, P. et al. (2017c). Introduction: The paradoxes of paradox. In W. K. Smith, M. W. Lewis, P. Jarzabkowski et al. (eds.), *The Oxford handbook of organizational paradox* (pp. 1–24). Oxford: Oxford University Press.

Smith, W. K., and Tracey, P. (2016). Institutional complexity and paradox theory: Complementarities of competing demands. *Strategic Organization* 14(4): 455–66.

Smith, W. K., and Tushman, M. L. (2005). Managing strategic contradictions: A top management model for managing innovation streams. *Organization Science* 16(5): 522–36.

Sparr, J. L. (2018). Paradoxes in organizational change: The crucial role of leaders' sensegiving. *Journal of Change Management* 18(2): 162–80.

Stacey, R. D. (1996). *Complexity and creativity in organizations*. San Francisco: Berrett-Koehler.

Stephenson, K. A., Kuismin, A., Putnam, L. L. et al. (2020). Process studies of organizational space. *Academy of Management Annals* 14(2): 797–827.

Sterman, J. D. (1994). Learning in and about complex systems. *System Dynamics Review* 10(2–3): 291–330.

Sunstein, C. R. (2020). Sludge audits. *Behavioural Public Policy*. 1–20. https://doi.org/10.1017/bpp.2019.32.

Takeuchi, H., Osono, E. and Shimizu, N. (2008). The contradictions that drive Toyota's success. *Harvard Business Review* June: 96–104.

Taylor, F. W. (1911). *Scientific management*. New York: Norton.

Tett, G. (2015). *The silo effect: The peril of expertise and the promise of breaking down barriers*. New York: Simon and Schuster.

Tsoukas, H. (2018). From agility to antifragility: Coping with the unknowable. In C. Prange and L. Heracleous (eds.), *Agility X: How organizations thrive in unpredictable times* (pp. 43–53). Cambridge: Cambridge University Press.

Tsoukas, H., and Cunha, M. P. (2017). On organizational circularity: Vicious and virtuous circles in organizing. In M. W. Lewis, W. K. Smith, P. Jarzabkowski and A. Langley (eds.), *The Oxford handbook of organizational paradox: Approaches to plurality, tensions, and contradictions* (pp. 393–412). New York: Oxford University Press.

Tuckermann, H. (2019). Visibilizing and invisibilizing paradox: A process study of interactions in a hospital executive board. *Organization Studies* 40(12): 1851–72.

Tzu, L. (2011). *Tao te ching: A book about the way and the power of the way*. Boston, MA: Shambala.

Van Gansbeke, F. (2021). Sustainability and the downfall of Danone CEO Faber (1 and 2) *Forbes*. 20 March. www.forbes.com/sites/frankvangans

beke/2021/03/20/sustainability-and-the-downfall-of-danone-ceo-faber-12/? sh=1b1208775b16. Accessed 28 July 2021.

Vignehsa, K. (2014). *The art of stuckedness: When practices persist against all odds*. PhD, University of Technology Sydney.

Vince, R., and Broussine, M. (1996). Paradox, defense and attachment: Accessing and working with emotions and relations underlying organizational change. *Organization Studies* 17(1): 1–21.

Vuori, T. O., and Huy, Q. N. (2016). Distributed attention and shared emotions in the innovation process: How Nokia lost the smartphone battle. *Administrative Science Quarterly* 61(1): 9–51.

Watzlawick, P., Jackson, D. D. and Bavelas, J. B. (1967). *Pragmatics of human communication: A study of interactional patterns, pathologies, and paradoxes*. New York: Norton.

Weick, K. E. (1979). *The social psychology of organizing*. Reading, MA: Addison-Wesley.

Weick, K. E. (1995) *Sensemaking in organizations*. Thousand Oaks, CA: Sage.

Wendt, R. F. (1995). Women in positions of service: The politicized body. *Communication Studies* 46(3–4): 276–96.

Westenholz, A. (1993). Paradoxical thinking and change in the frames of reference. *Organization Studies* 14(1): 37–58.

Whyte, W. H. (1956). *The organization man*. New York: Simon and Schuster

Wittgenstein, L. (2010). *Philosophical investigations*. London: John Wiley & Sons.

Zhao, S. (1991). Metatheory, metamethod, meta-data-analysis: What, why, and how? *Sociological Perspectives* 34(3): 377–90.

Zorina, A., Bélanger, F., Kumar, N. and Clegg, S. (2021). Watchers, watched, and watching in the digital age: Reconceptualization of information technology monitoring as complex action nets. *Organization Science* 32(6): 1571–96.

Cambridge Elements ☰

Organization Theory

Nelson Phillips

Imperial College London, University of Alberta

Nelson Phillips is the Abu Dhabi Chamber Professor of Strategy and Innovation at Imperial College London. His research interests include organization theory, technology strategy, innovation, and entrepreneurship, often studied from an institutional theory perspective.

Royston Greenwood

Imperial College London, University of Alberta

Royston Greenwood is the Telus Professor of Strategic Management at the University of Alberta, a visiting professor at the University of Cambridge, and a visiting professor at the University of Edinburgh. His research interests include organizational change and professional misconduct.

About the Series

Organization theory covers many different approaches to understanding organizations. Its focus is on what constitutes the how and why of organizations and organizing, bringing understanding of organizations in a holistic way. The purpose of Elements in Organization Theory is to systematize and contribute to our understanding of organizations.

Cambridge Elements $^{\equiv}$

Organization Theory

Printed in the United States
by Baker & Taylor Publisher Services